# Leavenworth Papers
## Number 19

# Scenes from an Unfinished War: Low-Intensity Conflict in Korea, 1966—1969

by Major Daniel P. Bolger

Combat Studies Institute
U.S. Army Command and General Staff College
Fort Leavenworth, Kansas 66027-6900

# Contents

Illustrations .................................................... v
Tables .......................................................... vii
Preface ......................................................... ix
Introduction .................................................... xi
Chapter
   1. The Land of the Morning Calm ............................. 1
   2. Concrete Actions ........................................ 33
   3. A Continuous Nightmare .................................. 61
   4. Isolated Provocations ................................... 89
   5. What Went Right ........................................ 111
Appendix 1. The Second Korean Conflict—
           A Chronology of Key Events ........................ 127
Appendix 2. U.S. Forces, Korea, Order of Battle, 1 January 1968 ...... 131
Appendix 3. Annex 1, Tactical Disposition of Korean People's Army
           Maneuver Forces, 1 January 1968 ..................... 133
           Annex 2, Tactical Disposition of U.S. Eighth Army
           Maneuver Forces, 1 January 1968 ..................... 135
Appendix 4. Significant U.S.-KPA Firefights, November
           1966—December 1969 ................................. 137
Notes ........................................................... 141
Glossary ........................................................ 153
Bibliography .................................................... 155

# Illustrations

## Figures

1. United Nations Command-U.S. Forces, Korea-U.S. Eighth Army operational chains of command .................. 6
2. United States' objectives in Korea, 1966—69 .................. 11
3. Korean People's Army and associated forces along the U.S.-held segment of the DMZ, 1 January 1968 .................. 16
4. DPRK campaign plan (new military line), announced 5—12 October 1966 .................. 34
5. The spectrum of conflict in Korea, 1966—69 .................. 43
6. UNC anti-infiltration dispositions (idealized example) .................. 48
7. U.S. maneuver battalion DMZ training and rotation plan .................. 54
8. The United States' military response to the seizure of the USS *Pueblo*, January through March 1968 .................. 72
9. American maneuver battalion deployment as of 30 April 1969 (typical after 21 March 1968) .................. 81
10. U.S. combat forces deployed for Exercise Focus Retina, March 1969 .................. 99
11. The United States' response to the downing of the EC-121M, April 1969 .................. 106
12. DMZ incidents involving casualties to U.S. forces (since 3 December 1969) .................. 125

## Maps

1. Korea, 1966—69 .................. 19
2. The DMZ, U.S. sector, 1966—69 .................. 22

# Tables

1. Balance of conventional military power in Korea, November 1966 .................................................... 14
2. Strength of U.S. divisions in Korea, 1 January 1968 ................ 26
3. The Second Korean Conflict: A statistical summary, 1966–69 ...... 112
4. Republic of Korea population and gross national product, 1962–72 ..................................................... 114

# *Preface*

When I was a young lieutenant, a battle-wise infantry officer named Colonel Walter B. Clark told me about a war that most Americans, including me, had never heard about. At the time, I listened to his stories with interest; there were so many provocative ideas and useful lessons to be considered, even for an inexperienced soldier. At one point in our discussions, I recall saying to the colonel that some day, someone should tell the story of this second Korean war.

This is my attempt to tell that story in a way that professional soldiers might find useful. I make no pretense of providing the complete account of the undeclared, unconventional struggle that gripped Korea between 1966 and 1969, although this effort may serve to refocus attention on a most intriguing chapter in the annals of American and Korean arms. Accordingly, this work is dedicated to Colonel Clark and all the other American and Korean veterans of the Second Korean Conflict. I would like also to thank Dr. Samuel Lewis, Dr. Lawrence A. Yates, Dr. Robert Berlin, Mr. Don Gilmore, and the diligent CSI staff for their kind assistance in this project.

# *Introduction*

> ... this strategy would involve us in the wrong war, at the wrong place, at the wrong time, and with the wrong enemy.
>
> — Omar N. Bradley
> General of the Army,
> May 1951

Can Americans fight a successful counterguerrilla war? Thirty years ago, most American soldiers would have answered "yes." The more historically minded might have justified that assertion by pointing to decades of U.S. Indian fighting, years in the Philippines battling Moros and Huks, several Marine Corps "Banana Wars" in Latin America, and the successful anti-Communist struggle in post-1945 Greece. "Any good soldier can handle guerrillas," Army Chief of Staff General George H. Decker told President John F. Kennedy.[1] Kennedy and his brain trust decided to test Decker's claim in a place called Vietnam.

America's leaders, however, failed in their confused, tragic confrontation with insurgency in Southeast Asia—with plenty of blame to spare for all involved. A consensus emerged, both in the armed forces and in the wider body of interested citizenry: U.S. troops could not, would not, and should not become involved in any situations variously termed as counterguerrilla, cold war, counterinsurgency, stability, or (the current favorite) low-intensity conflict (LIC).

This idea persists virtually unchallenged. Contemporary operations in El Salvador, Panama, and the Philippines notwithstanding, few American professional soldiers have much stomach for counterguerrilla fighting. In a recent study, a high-level joint-service team concluded: "The United States does not understand low-intensity conflict nor does it display the capability to adequately defend against it."[2] LIC is the "wrong war" for Americans and Vietnam *seemed* the proof that brooked no argument.

Still, the argument needs to be pursued, as its very premise may be based too much on one sad case. Accepting for the moment that Vietnam was indeed largely an insurgency (a contentious matter in its own right), one can still take issue with prevailing opinions. Does Vietnam prove that Americans cannot conduct successful LIC?

Before confronting this issue, it is critical to get definitions straight. Low-intensity conflict is war, deadly as any, but different in that its adherents stress the achievement of political goals by insurgency, terrorism, and provocation rather than traditional force-on-force military operations. Small countries can risk such bold efforts, even against the great powers and their allies, thanks to the paralyzing effects of the U.S.-USSR nuclear stalemate.

Nuclear weaponry places a definite brake on the superpowers. No matter how vital the interests involved, it is important for the superpowers to keep confrontations localized and small in scale, lest the United States and Soviet Union slip from confrontation into the maelstrom of high-intensity nuclear war. For superpowers, *severely limited means*, rather than limited ends, distinguish LIC from midintensity struggles. Means are now the only real variable; wars of unlimited aims are no longer much of an option for nuclear giants.

That explains why these shadow wars have found such favor among minor states. In their seemingly endless jockeying for advantage under the frustrating nuclear standoff, both superpowers have routinely backed their enemy's enemies. This has only strengthened the hands of determined local belligerents. A well-prosecuted guerrilla movement or terror campaign places an involved great power on the horns of a dilemma: should the great power increase its aims and risk nuclear war against the small power's sponsor or increase its means and risk diversions from more important areas?

America's adversaries have a built-in edge in that the Soviet Union and its allies espouse anti-American insurrection as a matter of basic philosophy. By Marxist lights, struggling against the capitalist United States is inevitable, and so adherents of communism have sound theoretical and practical foundations to support their fight. As America discovered in Africa, Asia, and Latin America, Communist ideology, in both its Leninist and Maoist strains, provides an especially potent blueprint for countries interested in engaging and defeating the United States in a protracted struggle.

From the American perpective, LIC occurs when the U.S. military seeks limited aims with a relatively modest number of available regular forces. The "low" aspect of LIC refers directly to the degree of American commitment (certainly not to the level of violence or degree of enemy commitment). A few selected U.S. reserves may participate, but there is essentially no mobilization. Even a partial mobilization, whether formal (as in the Korean War) or informal (as in Vietnam), elevates the conflict to the midintensity realm, with all the resultant political hazards both at home and abroad.

Given this comprehensive definition, LIC necessarily comprises more than counterinsurgency. It entails almost any restrained use of U.S. military force to advance its interests in the Third World, to include peacekeeping, combating terrorism, and handling peacetime contingencies.[3] Yet it is typical of the rather muddled views on this subject that many experts employ the terms "LIC" and "counterinsurgency" interchangeably. Whatever the Vietnam experience suggests about U.S. abilities to battle insurgents, it offers little insight into American capacities for peacekeeping, fighting terrorists, or handling a diverse grab bag of "contingencies" (i.e., everything from punitive bombings and rescue efforts to shows of force).

Even focusing on counterinsurgency, the historical record still does not support the commonplace pessimism about recent U.S. military performance. Vietnam was only one of several American counterguerrilla wars of the 1960s. U.S. operations in the Congo (1960—65), Thailand (1964—74), the Dominican Republic (1965—66), and Bolivia (1966—67) proceeded and concluded differently than the Vietnam War. Some work has been done to resurrect interest in these unique small wars, but in general, they have been forgotten in the continuing fascination with the much more massive, conventional, and unsuccessful Southeast Asian undertaking.

Perhaps the most interesting "other" LIC of the 1960s occurred in Korea. There, an understrength, conventionally trained force of Americans, in company with their Republic of Korea (ROK) allies, fought and won a low-intensity war on the Asian mainland. There was nothing unusual about the soldiers involved: the unusual thing proved to be the imaginative, thoughtful ways in which they were used.

The Second Korean Conflict flared up in November 1966. By the time it sputtered to an ill-defined end more than three years later, the Democratic People's Republic of Korea had challenged the allies in every category of low-intensity conflict and failed. One would think that this case might merit a great deal of study—if only as a possible counterpoint to the usual litany of lessons about Vietnam.

Yet to understand why the Second Korean Conflict has been so rarely addressed, one would do well to return to Bradley's quotation. Only in this case, one must give a new twist to Bradley. Korea in 1968—69 was again the wrong war, but this time, it was wrong in a different way.

First, unlike the earlier war, the war in Korea in 1966—69 was not a conventional, stand-up war. By standard American doctrine, it was all wrong. The sporadic combat mainly devolved upon the ROK forces and population. While American leaders made most of the key decisions and provided certain absolutely critical combat forces and battlefield multipliers, the ROKs did the overwhelming bulk of the work. Shrewd U.S. officers ensured that the ROKs got the credit for decisions and plans, too. This was right and proper for a LIC environment, but it did not make for much popular excitement in the United States, especially compared with the concurrent American big-unit war in Vietnam.

Second, Korea was no more the preferred battlefield in the late 1960s than it had been in 1951. Korea constituted an economy-of-force theater. The "right place" was Southeast Asia. American commanders in Korea faced the difficult prospect of defending their area without daring to engender a second major Asian war. Only if the U.S. generals erred would they garner any special notice. The more they succeeded, the less attention they received. By the time it became evident that the Second Korean Conflict had been won, it was equally obvious that the Vietnam War had been lost. Interest focused there and has remained so ever since.

Thus, the Second Korean Conflict has drifted into obscurity, a curious episode, a footnote to the Vietnam era. In light of the ongoing LIC debate, this Korean experience deserves exhumation and examination. Because smart U.S. commanders risked fighting the "wrong kind" of war in Korea from 1966—69, the situation did not boil up into the other wrong kind of war everyone feared most—the dreaded second land war in Asia. Thus, the story of the Second Korean Conflict is the story of a wrong war that turned out right.

# The Land of the Morning Calm

> Weapons are tools of ill omen.
>
> —Sun-tzu
> Chinese military theorist,
> ca. 350 B.C.

## Background

The Korean Armistice Agreement of 27 July 1953 suspended large-scale conventional fighting in Korea after more than three years of bloody warfare. This instrument, "purely military in character" by its own verbiage, sought to "insure a complete cessation of hostilities and of all acts of armed forces in Korea until a final peaceful settlement [was] achieved."[1] The 1954 Geneva Conference ended without a political settlement on Korea. To date, only the most tentative steps have been taken toward peaceful resolution of the impasse.

During most of the decade after the armistice, both the North Korean Communists and the Republic of Korea continued to press claims for reunification under their respective banners. Premier Kim Il-sung of the Democratic People's Republic of Korea (DPRK) presented many proposals for a united peninsula, each predicated upon termination of the existing South Korean government. President Syngman Rhee preferred to talk of "unification by marching northward." Each Korea rejected the other's plans.[2] Due to wartime damage and the moderating influence of their powerful Chinese and American allies, neither the north nor the south attempted to take serious steps toward implementing their reunification schemes.

This relatively stable situation began to change by the start of the second postwar decade. For both Koreas, but especially for the militant north, the mid-1960s represented a period of particular opportunities and perils. A succession of interrelated events in the two states laid the foundation for the Second Korean Conflict.

In the DPRK, the departure of the Chinese People's Volunteer Army by October 1958 gave Kim Il-sung a free hand to do things his way. Thus, he completed the consolidation of his domestic authority in a series of discrete purges in the upper echelons of his Korean Workers' Party (KWP). Kim followed the Chinese model for his *Chollima* (Flying Horse) plan, a crash program of collectivized agriculture and forced industrialization. His goal, simply stated, was "the fortification of the entire country" as a base for reunifying Korea by force.

But Kim could not do the job alone. He needed advanced Soviet technology and advice to build a powerful industrial state, but he depended on the Chinese for more immediate agricultural assistance. Reliance on these two sources became especially difficult in light of the increasingly heated disagreements between the two Communist giants. Like the rest of the lesser Communist states, the DPRK felt pressured to take a side in the ideological bickering between Nikita S. Khrushchev of the USSR and Mao Zedong (Mao Tse-tung) of China.

Given North Korea's pivotal geographic position, recent role in the struggle against the Americans, and economic requirements, Kim Il-sung could not afford to alienate either of his mighty sponsors. Although he attempted to chart a middle course, he failed. The Soviets suspended aid to him in December 1962, charging that the DPRK had leaned too far toward the Chinese.[3]

While Kim Il-sung tried to build a mobilization base with the help of squabbling allies, Syngman Rhee of the ROK dealt with his own challenges. Aid from the United States and other United Nations countries allowed

Premier Kim Il-sung of the Democratic People's Republic of Korea

South Korea to rebuild rapidly. Its gross national product grew at an annual rate of 5.5 percent during the mid-1950s. Industry led the way, expanding at an astounding 14 percent yearly. The elderly Rhee proved unable to cope with the social upheavals caused by this economic upsurge. Charged with electoral corruption in April 1960, Rhee resigned in the face of widespread civil disorder, popularized as the Student Revolution.

Following a brief, confused period of rule by fragmented opposition factions, Major General Park Chung Hee assumed power through a coup d'état in May 1961. Park and his junta exercised supreme powers until August 1963, when Park was elected president. Despite the political turnover, the ROK economy continued to burgeon, led by the industrial sector.[4]

What did the northern Communist leadership make of these developments? As far as can be told from available open sources, Kim Il-sung drew three conclusions as early as December 1962. First, the ROK economy and population were already twice as large as those of North Korea. Obvious trend lines indicated that the disparity, especially in the economic realm, would increase over time. Second, the Park government represented a unique threat. Although nominally "civil" after the 1963 elections, Park and his circle of military men could be expected to display strategic vision far beyond that of the Rhee administration. Park's emphasis on accelerated industrial growth underscored his commitment to military strength. In league with the ROK's already expanding economic advantage over the DPRK, Park's calculated catalysis of industry promised to furnish the means for South Korea to conduct the march to the north so often threatened by Rhee. Third, the economic boom in the south had spawned serious dissent in the Republic of Korea. In 1960—61, the DPRK had been unready to exploit the unsettled situation or take direct action.[5] Because the Soviet aid needed for conventional combat was suspended, Kim Il-sung wondered if there was an opportunity for him to bring about reunification through unconventional war.

Kim thought so. On 10 December 1962, he propounded a new "military line" to the Fifth Plenum of the KWP's Central Committee. Kim's ideas were somewhat original, but the tone was definitely Maoist. Because the Soviet Union had temporarily cut Kim Il-sung adrift, this embrace of some aspects of Chinese thought was not surprising. More to the point, Maoist guerrilla concepts suited what Kim considered to be the "objective circumstances" on the Korean peninsula.

Kim advocated a politically aware "army of cadres" (revolutionary agitators), the arming of his entire populace, completion of nationwide military industrialization, and modernization of his conventional armed forces. Rejecting his army's almost wholly conventional Soviet-style doctrine, the DPRK premier directed an emphasis on irregular warfare drawn from studies of his own operations against the Japanese during World War II. Finally, he began to manipulate key party and military appointments to favor his former guerrilla comrades, the Kapsan faction.[6]

President Park Chung Hee of South Korea

Kim ordered immediate agitation-propaganda efforts to throw sand into the gears of ROK progress while he created his new unconventional military machine. He demanded fast action, but even so, he anticipated that it might take until the completion of the current Seven Year Plan (1960—67) for the DPRK to be fully ready for an unconventional campaign.[7]

Events of 1965—66 caused Kim Il-sung to accelerate his timetable. ROK diplomatic and military initiatives served notice that the south no longer felt mortally threatened by its Communist northern neighbor. When President Park signed a treaty with Japan in 1965, the Republic of Korea publicly entered the community of Asian states. This normalized relations between the South Koreans and their former overlords, with Japan finally recognizing an independent ROK. With this recognition came greatly increased Japanese loans, investments, and trade—all fueling the already humming ROK economic engine.

In the wake of this Japanese agreement, President Park moved to consolidate his country's position as an emerging Asian power. In June 1966, he hosted the Asian Pacific Council (Taiwan, Japan, Malaysia, the Philippines, South Vietnam, Thailand, Australia, and Laos) in Seoul. It seemed like a "coming out party" for the ROK. Diplomatic recognition of South Korea doubled during 1966.

A month later, Park's government signed a Status of Forces Agreement with the United States. For the first time, the two countries treated each other as equals at the bargaining table. A United Nations Command (UNC) headquarters team studied ways to reflect this new relationship in the U.S.-dominated military chain of command in Korea.[8]

These diplomatic achievements signaled that Park's improvements were already bearing valuable fruit. The DPRK could not wait until 1967 to act. Fortunately for the North Koreans, the second major development of those years provided what looked like an opening for a serious effort to destabilize the south. In March 1965, the United States deployed ground forces into South Vietnam, thereby joining that forlorn war. By September of that same year, ROK Army units had joined their American allies in Vietnam. Park dispatched some 46,000 ROK soldiers and marines, with the final contingent under way on 15 October 1966.[9] The Korean forces provided substantial combat power to the allied endeavors in Southeast Asia.

From Kim Il-sung's perspective, however, this situation offered the chance he needed. While he knew that the ROK forces would certainly benefit from combat experience and issues of new American weaponry, he also recognized an important military point: for the first time since 1953, the Republic of Korea had divided its military effort. The fact that the United States had at last turned its sights to another Asian country also might benefit the DPRK.[10] Even as the last few men of the ROK 9th "White Horse" Infantry Division left for Vietnam, Kim Il-sung decided to act. To the south, the Americans and their Korean allies maintained their lonely, boring vigil. The Second Korean Conflict was about to begin.

## *Organization*

To appreciate the American-ROK performance in the fighting of 1966—69, one must begin with an understanding of the overall military organizational structure. "Convoluted" might be the kindest term describing the chain of command in Korea. There were actually two major chains, one for combined U.S.-ROK operations and the other primarily concerned with U.S. joint-service efforts (see figure 1).

The United Nations Command, a combined headquarters, existed as a legacy of the Korean War. In accordance with the July 1950 Security Council decision, the United States acted as the executive power for United Nations military interests in Korea. UNC operated directly under the supervision of the U.S. secretary of defense and the coordination of the Joint Chiefs of Staff (JCS). Although he did not hold precisely the same status as a unified commander in chief like that of U.S. Pacific Command or U.S. European Command, Commander in Chief, UNC (CINCUNC), enjoyed direct access to the national command authorities through the JCS.

By 1966, the UNC seemed to be a symbolic entity. The U.S. troops in country, an oversized company from Thailand, and a few ceremonial squads comprised the only significant remnants of the multinational UN forces of

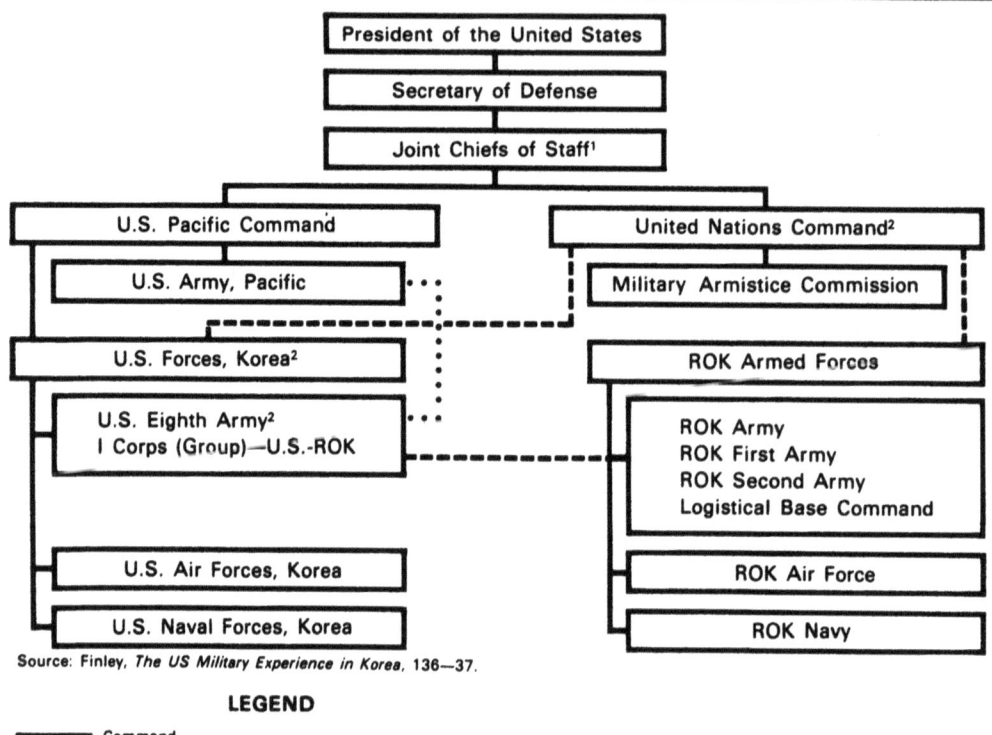

Source: Finley, *The US Military Experience in Korea*, 136–37.

**LEGEND**

──── Command
──── Operational control during wartime
•••• Administrative channel (command less operational control)

[1]The JCS by statute "assist the secretary" in his direction of U.S. armed forces. Although designated as a channel for communications only, the JCS in fact have often functioned, particularly in the 1960s, as an executive agent for the secretary of defense.

[2]These positions were held concurrently by the same officer, General Charles H. Bonesteel III.

Figure 1. United Nations Command-U.S. Forces, Korea-U.S. Eighth Army operational chains of command (as of 1 November 1968 but representative of the 1968–69 period)

1950—53, although in theory, the other participants would come back if war broke out again. The principal UN military activity in Korea involved participation in the interminable series of fruitless armistice meetings at Panmunjom.

The UNC mantle, however, gave its holder one important power. Since no formal peace treaty superseded the battlefield truce of 1953, UNC retained operational control over the ROK military, which had been granted by Syngman Rhee back in July 1950.[11] Thus, the American general who bore the title of CINCUNC could direct the tactical employment of ROK forces, even in the absence of overt, large-scale hostilities.

This degree of American authority over foreign forces contrasted markedly with the provisions in other theaters under U.S. command. In the North Atlantic Treaty Organization, the American serving as Supreme Allied Commander, Europe, commanded the vast bulk of his multinational fighting forces only in wartime—and then only if those units' parent countries chose to participate. In Southeast Asia, the Commander, U.S. Military Assistance Command, Vietnam, exercised no formal powers over the South Vietnamese armed forces.[12] While U.S. commanders in Europe and Vietnam had access to far more powerful forces than the Commander in Chief, UNC, the American general in Korea actually directed his combined organization.

The joint-service United States Forces, Korea (USFK) plugged into the second major chain of command in the theater. USFK functioned as a subordinate unified command under the U.S. Pacific Command. The USFK headquarters commanded all American land (U.S. Eighth Army), air, and sea forces on the Korean peninsula proper. It exercised no authority over the U.S. Seventh Fleet in the waters around Korea, nor could it command the U.S. Fifth Air Force in the airspaces adjacent to Korea. All was fine as long as conditions in Korea conformed to those envisioned when the UN joined the war in 1950. In that case, UNC commanded USFK and the ROK armed forces.

It took no great imagination to conceive of conditions in Korea that might entail the use of armed forces outside the purview of the United Nations. These included certain routine peacetime exercises, bilateral U.S.-ROK concerns like Vietnam, incidents of interest only to the United States or the ROK, or a new Korean war that did not concern the steadily more radical rank-and-file states of the UN General Assembly. In those all too likely cases, USFK reverted to U.S. Pacific Command control. Yet operations outside the UNC structure forfeited the advantage of U.S. operational control over the ROK military, leaving the allies to hash out these delicate matters, perhaps in the teeth of a crisis or even a full-blown war.

The United States military evolved a clever solution to this potential quandary: giving one man multiple "hats" (posts). The *same* U.S. Army four-star general concurrently held the posts of Commander in Chief, United Nations Command; Commander of U.S. Forces, Korea; and Commanding General, U.S. Eighth Army (EUSA). Regardless of the nature of events in Korea, this ensured that USFK complied with the immediate needs of UNC rather than the distant Pacific Command (PACOM). In his capacity as Commander in Chief, UNC, this general assigned operational control of the ROK Army to the Commanding General, EUSA (himself).[13]

Even with this neat bureaucratic trick, some problems remained. First, the U.S. commander had operational control over his combined and joint U.S. forces (through his UNC and USFK hat). These elements answered to the U.S. general for task organization and tactical missions but *not* for administration, discipline, internal organization, or unit training.[14] The American general could use the capabilities of the forces, but he could only do so much to create new capabilities or modify old ones in his combined and joint units. The exception, of course, was his own outfit, U.S. Eighth Army.

Second, PACOM component headquarters (U.S. Army, Pacific; U.S. Pacific Air Forces; U.S. Pacific Fleet) had authority to bypass UNC and exercise administrative control over their service elements in U.S. Forces, Korea. Such control meant the ability to dictate allocations of trained men and valuable equipment.[15] This became problematic as these headquarters sought to divert maximum resources to the ongoing war in Vietnam.

The U.S. Army four-star general could deal with the steady spate of Army requisitions, thanks to his concurrent UNC-USFK-EUSA roles and consequent direct access to the JCS and the secretary of defense. But the American commander's air and naval subordinates had no such luxury, and USFK could not help them much due to the limits implied by operational control. As a result, with only junior flag officers to shield them, the U.S. Navy and U.S. Air Force contributions in Korea grew more and more hollow as the Vietnam War dragged on.

Finally, along with his three principal hats, the senior U.S. Army general in Korea performed several other important duties. He supervised the extensive U.S. military advisory and assistance program (which fell under the ambassador's control in most other countries). He also provided military expertise to the U.S. ambassador in Seoul. In addition, he presented military opinions and ideas to the president of the ROK and his ministers. These added responsibilities could give a smart U.S. commander important leverage over the U.S. embassy staff and ROK politicians. At times, however, each of the extra roles threatened to turn into full-time jobs and divert attention from the general's three other equally full-time commands.

The U.S. organization in Korea was hardly ideal, but it promised a clever, hard-working commander one absolutely vital attribute: unity of command—if he had the drive and talents to exercise it. Under the usual circumstances, a U.S. general commanding the Korean theater could hope to muddle through, focusing on whatever jobs he did best and leaving the rest to good deputies and chiefs of staff. But the years 1966 through 1969 were not marked by usual circumstances.

Luckily for the U.S.-ROK side, General Charles H. "Tick" Bonesteel III turned out to be a man as unusual as his times demanded. Bonesteel, a fourth-generation West Point graduate (class of 1931) and son of a general, served in World War II as a staff engineer and operations planner at army group and War Department level. In Washington, Bonesteel worked with the rising stars of America's power elite, including an old Oxford University roommate, a wartime colonel named Dean Rusk. By odd coincidence, Bonesteel was one of those who selected the 38th parallel to divide Korea for what was presumed to be temporary postwar occupation by Soviet and American troops.

After 1945, Bonesteel helped administer the economic recovery of postwar Europe, served with the Department of State and the National Security Council, and performed strategic planning as a special assistant to the chairman of the Joint Chiefs of Staff. After a brief stint as commanding general of a division and a corps stationed in Germany, he returned to

General Charles H. Bonesteel III, Commander in Chief, United Nations Command; Commander, U.S. Forces, Korea; Commander, U.S. Eighth Army

Washington as director of special studies for the U.S. Army chief of staff. He also represented the United States on the United Nations Military Staff Committee.[16] Despite these sterling credentials, Bonesteel lacked combat experience.

Perhaps because of his repeated high-level staff tours, he did not display any intuitive sense for inspiring soldiers. Indeed, many who knew him stated that he felt awkward talking to enlisted soldiers and so avoided visiting units in the field. Although tall, gray haired, thin, and sporting a rakish eye patch over his left eye (the result of a detached retina), Bonesteel did little to capitalize on his imposing patrician appearance. Impressing his troops simply was not important to him. "I used to have to drag him off to get a haircut; otherwise he'd just let it grow," an officer on his personal staff recalled.[17] In brief, Bonesteel was no Patton.

Still, his lack of charismatic leadership mattered little, partly because his position did not require such displays, but mainly because his other abilities proved so formidable. Bonesteel possessed a brilliant mind, honed by his education at Oxford as a Rhodes Scholar and broadened by his unusual assignments.[18] He knew a lot, but more important, he knew how to use his store of data for creative thinking.

Bonesteel displayed five distinct intellectual talents. Any one of these abilities would have marked him as an extraordinary officer. Together, these traits suited him admirably for his demanding role in Korea and marked him as a rarity in the U.S. Army. Of his contemporaries, only a handful of men, such as Andrew J. Goodpaster, Bernard Rogers, George M. Seignious, and Vernon Walters, displayed similar political-military prowess.

First, Bonesteel could process an immense amount of information in a short time. Like Napoleon Bonaparte, Bonesteel showed a flair for juggling his many duties. He had the mental discipline to do several things at once and yet keep them straight in his mind. Without this skill, he would have been unable to use the full range of powers granted to him by his three hats.

Second, from the seemingly discordant mass of incoming information that came to him daily, Bonesteel repeatedly discerned subtle connections. Similar to Frederick the Great, Bonesteel often proved his own best analyst of this influx of intelligence. He refused to be limited by the circumscribed military information delivered by his dutiful intelligence staff. As he put it, he "swung the bolo knife around a bit" and "tried to put intelligence on a more direct basis."[19] Bonesteel requested and received a plethora of raw political, economic, social, and personal details. Working with his typically blinding speed, he drew his own conclusions. He was almost always correct.

Third, Bonesteel demonstrated impressive political acumen. His informed perception gave him an uncanny sense for the delicate political-military balances that constrain the operational level of war. He recognized the difference between the possible and the ideal, and he declined to prejudice the former while pursuing the latter.[20] In this, he resembled General Matthew Ridgway, although Bonesteel went well beyond that estimable old soldier with regard to achieving maximum cooperation from the Republic of Korea. Bonesteel was always able to do more with less, so much so that harried superiors occasionally expected him to do everything with nothing.

Fourth, Bonesteel embraced the unorthodox. Probably due to his own atypical professional experience, he did not feel bound by traditional U.S. Army doctrine, practices, or customs. In this, he resembled such self-educated soldiers as Daniel Morgan or Nathan Bedford Forrest. Bonesteel emphasized "good old-fashioned horse sense" instead of doctrinal rules or high technology. "I was anxious to get ideas from anybody," said Bonesteel, "from a shoe black to a senior officer, or anybody else."[21] This attitude allowed Bonesteel to meet unique challenges with unique solutions.

Finally, making hard choices is the hallmark of able generals from Alexander to Douglas MacArthur. In the words of his aide, Bonesteel "knew how to make decisions, and he made them without hesitation."[22] This ability permitted the general to translate his brilliance into positive actions. The Second Korean Conflict required a man willing to use the full range of formal and informal political-military powers available to him. When General Bonesteel took charge of his three commands on 1 September 1966, he had both the authority and the inclination to act as an American proconsul.

## *Mission*

Bonesteel and his U.S.-ROK combined forces had one clear strategic objective: defense of the Republic of Korea (see figure 2). Until late 1966, that implied defense against a repetition of the June 1950 invasion from the north. Since any big invasion would come by land through the Demilitarized Zone (DMZ), alertness in carrying out armistice duties appeared to offer some chance at early warning. In the meantime, the allies did their part to uphold the UN part of the cease-fire agreement. If U.S.-ROK guards in the DMZ and ROK coastal patrols could scoop up an occasional infiltrator from the north in the process, so much the better.

Unconventional war did not appear to be a special danger. True, both Koreas probed and tested each other, but they generally restricted their

---

Strategic objective: Defend the Republic of Korea against aggression by the Democratic Republic of Korea (North Korea).

Operational objectives:
- Defend against conventional invasion.
- Defend against unconventional operations/insurgencies.
  — Anti-infiltration (DMZ/coast).
  — Counterinsurgency (interior).

Strategic objectives:
- Restrain Republic of Korea actions.
- Conduct operations in an economy-of-force role (do not dilute the U.S. Vietnam War effort).

Sources: United States Army, 2d Infantry Division, "Operational Report—Lessons Learned, Headquarters, 2d Infantry Division, Period Ending 30 April 1969 (U)," UNCLASSIFIED, 1—2; General Charles H. Bonesteel III, United States Army (ret.), Interview with Lieutenant Colonel Robert St. Louis, 333—34, Senior Officers Oral History Program Project 73-2, 1973, United States Army Military History Institute, Carlisle Barracks, PA; and Trevor Armbrister, *A Matter of Accountability: The True Story of the Pueblo Affair* (New York: Coward McCann, 1970), 275—77.

---

Figure 2. United States' objectives in Korea, 1966—69

actual penetrations to intelligence-gathering efforts. Bonesteel characterized these northern agents as the "cornball military intelligence type, writing down the names of units from signs over the entrance gate and so on." A few firefights had erupted when such spies ran into ROK and U.S. forces. On the whole, however, casualties since the Korean War had been minimal.[23] Had anyone been in the mind to notice, they might have charted a small but important upsurge in violent incidents throughout 1965 and into 1966.

The defense of the ROK against midintensity and low-intensity threats carried one dangerous contradiction. If confronted with unconventional pressures, the U.S.-ROK combined forces would undoubtedly turn to meet the new problems. The allies had to be careful, though, lest their zest for low-intensity conflict undermine their capacities to resist a conventional invasion. By the same token, excessive unwillingness to alter conventional defense postures in order to meet and stop unconventional enemies might allow DPRK agitators to create enough instability to subvert the ROK government. Bonesteel would have to be very discriminating in handling LIC situations. Ultimately, he would have to create the proper combination of defenses, or Korea might collapse into war or anarchy.

America's strategic aim in Korea did not make Bonesteel's task any easier. With its forces fully engaged in Vietnam, the United States wished to prevent a renewal of the Korean War. The ROKs, hoping for eventual reunification, only grudgingly shared this American strategic objective. Senior U.S. officers rarely discussed this issue in public for fear of alienating their ROK counterparts, although the southern leaders certainly knew of the American concern; it pervaded all U.S.-ROK discussions about responses to North Korean provocations.

Bonesteel's responsibility weighed heavily on him. He knew that Americans preferred a quiet Korea—even if the country stayed divided. That might mean restraining the South Koreans, as Bonesteel understood. It also meant restraining himself. He vowed "not to take one damned thing from Vietnam."[24] The military term for this was "economy of force." Economy of force necessitates "the measured allocation of available combat power to the primary task as well as secondary tasks."[25] The United States had made its allocations of forces, and Korea played second fiddle to Vietnam. Bonesteel intended to keep it that way, even if it cost lives.

That, after all, loomed as the practical human price of an economy-of-force operation. Doctrine writers refer to the acceptance of "risk" in economy-of-force undertakings, implying the perils of casualties and possibly even defeat in the secondary arena. Bonesteel's men might have to suffer losses due to the lack of reinforcement simply to free up resources for the big war in Southeast Asia. At the operational level, economy of force risked reverses in the secondary theater. At the soldier level, it meant that young men risked death for no immediate, tangible gain. The cerebral Bonesteel needed to invent a way to defuse this potential morale problem, both for his own restive draftees and the aggressive ROKs.

The two missions in Korea did not necessarily work against each other as long as North Korea restrained itself. But that depended on Kim Il-sung's intentions; his capabilities to make trouble were not in doubt.

## *Enemy*

In evaluating the DPRK armed forces, one must be careful to distinguish between conventional and unconventional components. Prior to the final months of 1966, most U.S.-ROK collection and analysis focused upon the line units of the North Korean military. Kim Il-sung's new LIC forces had yet to show themselves in a major way.

The DPRK conventional order of battle certainly demanded concern. The north disposed a strong army, a surprisingly good air force, a small navy, and an improving militia at the village level. The north's sluggish socialist economy had not performed well since about 1960, but Kim Il-sung supplemented native industry by taking care to gain military aid from at least one and usually both Communist giants. Thanks to the ouster of Khrushchev in late 1964, the USSR had chosen to renew arms shipments in May 1965. Kim Il-sung gladly incorporated the new Soviet hardware into his military.[26]

Of the four branches of the DPRK armed forces, the Korean People's Army (KPA) posed the most noteworthy conventional threat (see table 1). It deployed eight infantry divisions along the DMZ, backed by eight more infantry divisions, three motorized infantry divisions, a tank division, a collection of separate infantry and tank brigades and regiments, and about ten skeleton-strength reserve divisions. Altogether, and assuming mobilization, the KPA could place about thirty-four division equivalents in the field.

Reports of the time credited the tough KPA conscripts as being "well-equipped and highly dedicated." KPA officers, many veterans of the 1950—53 fighting, knew their jobs. Kim Il-sung trusted his army so much that, unlike the Soviet or Chinese forces, his KPA had no true political officers. Commanders led without fear of ideological oversight. This allowed them a degree of initiative not often seen in Communist armies. Schooled on a mixture of Soviet, Chinese, and home-grown doctrine, the KPA practiced regularly for an attack to the south. American analysts warned that KPA "organization and emphasis on mechanized strength [gave] it a capability of rapidly moving into a strong offensive role."[27]

The Korean People's Air Force (KPAF) also worried U.S. and ROK planners. The KPAF's inventory of jet aircraft included some 60 Il-28 light bombers and about 450 MiG-15 and MiG-17 fighter-bombers, all suited for ground attack. The Soviet-trained pilots seemed bellicose and competent: two interceptors damaged a USAF RB-47 reconnaissance jet in mid-1965. Briefed on this air armada, General Bonesteel pronounced it "formidable." He feared that a massive KPAF preemptive strike could destroy the smaller ROK air arm on the ground before U.S. air reinforcements arrived to even the balance.[28]

## TABLE 1
## Balance of Conventional Military Power in Korea, November 1966

|  | DPRK | UNC | (U.S. portion) |
|---|---|---|---|
| ARMED FORCES PERSONNEL | 386,000 | 675,000 | (55,000) |
| Army |  |  |  |
|     Soldiers | 345,000 | 600,000 | (50,000)[1] |
|     Special Operations Forces | 3,000 | 1,000 |  |
|     Border Guards | 26,000 | 39,000 |  |
|     Militia | 1,200,000 | none[2] |  |
|     Regular divisions | 24 | 22 | (2) |
|     Reserve divisions | 10[3] | 10 |  |
|     Tanks | 800 | 656 | (216) |
|     Other armored vehicles | 900 | 1,381 | (781) |
|     Artillery | 5,200 | 2,160 | (224) |
| Air Force |  |  |  |
|     Airmen | 30,000 | 28,000 | (5,000) |
|     Combat airplanes | 590 | 265 | (60) |
|     Helicopters | 20 | 65 | (58) |
| Navy |  |  |  |
|     Sailors | 9,000 | 17,450 | (450) |
|     Marines | 2,000 | 30,050 | (50) |
|     Destroyers/frigates | 0 | 7 |  |
|     Submarines | 4 | 0 |  |
|     Minor combatants | 79 | 30 |  |
|     Landing craft | 20 | 23 |  |
|     Auxiliaries | 34 | 12 |  |

[1] About 46,000 ROK troops (2 Army divisions, 1 Marine brigade) were deployed to Vietnam at this time. They have been included in this table, although they were not immediately available.

[2] The ROK Homeland Defense Reserve Force, totaling over 2 million people, was not formally organized until 13 April 1968.

[3] At this time, little public information had been released concerning DPRK reserve divisions. Some U.S. sources later estimated that the DPRK disposed from 10 to 17 low-strength mobilization divisions (roughly equivalent of ROK reserve units).

Sources: Institute for Strategic Studies, *The Military Balance, 1968—69* (London: Adlard and Son, 1968), 13, 38—39; Joseph S. Bermudez, Jr., *North Korean Special Forces* (Surrey, England: Jane's Publishing Co., 1988), 101, 161; Shelby L. Stanton, *Vietnam Order of Battle* (Washington, DC: U.S. News Books, 1981), 272—73; General Charles H. Bonesteel III, United States Army (ret.), "U.S.-South Korean Partnership Holds a Truculent North at Bay," *Army* 19 (October 1969): 61; and James P. Finley, *The US Military Experience in Korea, 1971—1982: In the Vanguard of ROK-US Relations* (San Francisco, CA: Command Historian's Office, Secretary Joint Staff, HQ., USFK/EUSA, 1983), 19—21.

Analysis assessed the little Korean People's Navy (KPN) as "primarily a coastal defense force." Its four Soviet-made W-class submarines, four Soviet-supplied Komar-class missile boats, and cluster of motor torpedo boats might hamper U.S.-ROK sea lines of communication in the Sea of Japan.[29] Most allied planners readily discounted this small naval force.

The Workers' and Peasants' Red Guard Militia, organized in response to Kim Il-sung's December 1962 call for arming the populace, provided a pervasive government presence throughout North Korea. This vast force of discharged conscripts, local auxiliaries, informers, party activists, and observers supported the regular army components by guaranteeing rear-area security and trained replacements.[30] The ubiquitous militia made U.S.-ROK infiltrations of the north extremely hazardous, thereby hampering human intelligence gathering. In concert with the Ministry of Internal Affairs, the militia also ensured loyalty in the Communist state.

Powerful as the North Korean forces appeared, when placed in the full context of the conventional balance on the peninsula, the Communists did not possess a militarily significant advantage in combat power. If Kim Il-sung chose to reunify his country by force, he confronted two important problems. First, even with increased Soviet and Chinese material aid, the DPRK could not sustain a long war against its more populous and prosperous neighbor. If the two Koreas fought, the DPRK had to try for a quick knockout. A war of attrition favored the richer south. Second, the DPRK could not count on intervention from China or the USSR to offset the almost assured American role in any major renewal of the fighting. The north had to assume that the United States would reinforce its forward-deployed units, first with air power, then sea power, and finally with land power. Again, this argued for a lightning strike, winning before the U.S. reinforcements arrived.

Given the standing conventional balance in 1966, however, Kim Il-sung's generals could not reasonably expect to succeed in a risky blitzkrieg. The sides were too evenly matched.[31] Something had to be done to undermine ROK strengths in favor of the DPRK. Kim's new "military line" promised a solution to the problem. In the words of a later American report, "the ultimate aim of these operations is to create as much trouble as possible in South Korea, including difficulties in our relationships with the South Koreans. When these 'preparation of the battle area' efforts have achieved sufficient success, then the regular forces may be used as required in order to complete the communization of the Korean peninsula."[32] Put simply, a well-orchestrated northern LIC effort might spark the insurgency necessary to divert U.S.-ROK forces and give the edge to Kim Il-sung's conventional military units.

The North Korean premier chaired the National Intelligence Committee that directed and approved all intelligence and proinsurgency activities. Its subordinate Cabinet Intelligence Committee coordinated, collated, and analyzed information gathered by the field agencies. The actual DPRK field units amounted to fewer than 3,000 men (and selected women agents). Their low numbers could be deceptive, however, since each skilled operator-agitator had the potential to choose, train, and supervise up to a hundred informants and guerrilla recruits. In this aspect, they resembled U.S. Special Forces (Green Berets).

The KWP Liaison Department controlled tactical employment of intelligence and unconventional efforts (see figure 3). Its own Military Section

Conventional forces emplaced just north of the DMZ (west to east)

  Elements, II Corps

    Elements, 6th Infantry Division
    Elements, 8th Infantry Division

  Elements, VII Corps

    Elements, 15th Infantry Division
    Elements, 45th Infantry Division

Conventional/unconventional forces in the DMZ (west to east)

  Two companies, 6th Infantry Division DMZ Police
  Two companies, 8th Infantry Division DMZ Police
  Two companies, 15th Infantry Division DMZ Police
  Two companies, 45th Infantry Division DMZ Police

Unconventional infiltration forces

  Liaison Department, Korean Workers' party

    Military Section

    Guerrilla Guidance Section

    General Political Bureau of the KPA

      Propaganda and Instigation Bureau
      Enemy Affairs Guidance Bureau

    Security Bureau

    Reconnaissance Bureau, KPA[1]

      124th Army Unit (at least 9 operational detachments)
      283d Army Unit
      17th Foot Reconnaissance Brigade

[1]The Reconnaissance Bureau had assumed the lead role in unconventional warfare by late 1966, although it remained formally under the supervision of the Liaison Bureau.

Sources: Bermudez, *North Korean Special Forces*, 8, 26—34, 63, 157; and Bonesteel interview, 329—30.

Figure 3. Korean People's Army and associated forces along the U.S.-held segment of the DMZ, 1 January 1968

conducted surveillance and staged incidents designed to subvert the South Korean military and police. The Guerrilla Guidance Section assisted and fomented insurgency in the ROK.

In addition to these organic sections, the KWP Liaison Department supervised infiltrators from the KPA General Political Bureau. This outfit ran the Propaganda and Instigation Bureau and the Enemy Affairs Guidance Bureau. The former bureau attempted to cause individual defections and unit dissatisfaction in the ROK military. The latter focused on psychological warfare to undermine the morale of both the ROKs and the Americans.

The KWP Liaison Department also coordinated those Ministry of Internal Affairs investigations that required hot pursuit or preemptive raids south of the DMZ. Although rare, these Security Bureau missions made it very hard for U.S. and ROK agents to find their way north or return.

The final subordinate bureau under the KWP Liaison Department was the Reconnaissance Bureau of the Ministry of Defense. This element provided the main striking arm for Kim Il-sung's unconventional warfare effort. It operated four Foot Reconnaissance Stations, one in support of each KPA corps on the DMZ. Each station controlled a small foot reconnaissance brigade responsible for collection of military intelligence along the DMZ. These brigades often escorted and covered infiltrators from other DPRK agencies.[33]

The Reconnaissance Bureau also controlled the 23d Amphibious Brigade, which employed specially made infiltration boats to work the ROK coastlines. Camouflaged to look and sound like run-down fishing boats, these carefully engineered craft contained hidden diesel engines capable of bursts of incredible speeds (0—40 knots in three minutes). Moreover, their cleverly rounded wooden hulls defied radar acquisition. It took bold sailors to bring these craft inshore. Although the KPN might not have made much of a fight against the U.S. Seventh Fleet, its array of small-boat skills enabled it to deliver sea raiders under the most adverse conditions.

At this time, the North Koreans did not employ airborne insertions. The reasons for ignoring this potentially useful method included a lingering respect for the wartime UN air supremacy, concern over the excellent U.S.-ROK early-warning net, a shortage of trained pilots and specialized transport aircraft, and the lack of any indigenous experience in parachute and airlanding operations. The KPAF had concentrated on air defense and ground attack, not special operations. As long as the DMZ and coasts remained relatively accessible, the DPRK neglected aerial infiltration means.[34]

A recoilless rifle position along the DMZ

In addition to its own units, the Reconnaissance Bureau had authority to draw on conventional KPA, KPAF, and KPN units for support of its missions. In the DMZ, for example, frontline KPA divisions assisted infiltrations and covered withdrawals, often with supporting fires. North Korean divisions made especially good use of their DMZ Police Companies (troops routinely stationed in the northern half of the zone in accordance with the 1953 Armistice Agreement). DMZ Police supplied the latest situation updates and provided guides as necessary.[35]

North Korean infiltrators depended upon stealth to breach the DMZ or the ROK seacoasts. Superbly trained, repeatedly rehearsed, and thoroughly indoctrinated, these special fighters displayed remarkable knowledge of demolitions, land navigation, and small-unit tactics. Most doubled as political agitators, ever ready to reeducate interested locals and spread Kim Il-sung's gospel to what were thought to be willing southern ears.

These men drilled at evasion. Their mission lay in the ROK rear, where they usually moved in small teams of two to twelve men. Because each member normally carried little beyond his Soviet PPSh submachine gun and some demolitions, the KPA teams lacked the firepower to slug it out with conventional units. They preferred flight to battle.

When in contact, however, they fought with cunning and aggressiveness. The infiltrators proved adept at arranging violent, immediate ambushes, breaking contact, or waiting patiently for pursuers to pass by—whichever technique best suited their tactical situation. If trapped, these North Koreans rarely surrendered, preferring suicide by hand grenade.[36] Man for man, the DPRK special forces soldiers of 1966–69 might have been the toughest opponents ever to face American soldiers.

Additional special operations units still on the drawing boards would soon arrive to augment Kim Il-sung's able clandestine warriors. Even without them, however, the northern Communists had created a potent instrument for guerrilla combat. American and ROK ignorance of these deadly new enemies only made their impact that much more effective.

## *Terrain*

The topography of the Republic of Korea has been described as a petrified "sea in a heavy gale" (see map 1). Hills and ridges proliferate, with the exception of some rolling lowlands near Seoul, the capital and largest city. The long, rugged chain of the Taebaek Mountains defines most of eastern Korea; its affiliated Chiri Massif greatly restricts movement in the southern portion of the ROK. Much of the forest that once covered Korea has disappeared, leaving underbrush and saplings behind to inhibit mobility. Two rivers, the Imjin along the DMZ and the Han near Seoul, lie athwart movement corridors from north to south.

Weather also affected mobility in Korea in the 1960s. The peninsula's temperate climate resembled that of New York state. Glutinous mud hampered vehicle operations during the early spring thaw and the heavy rains

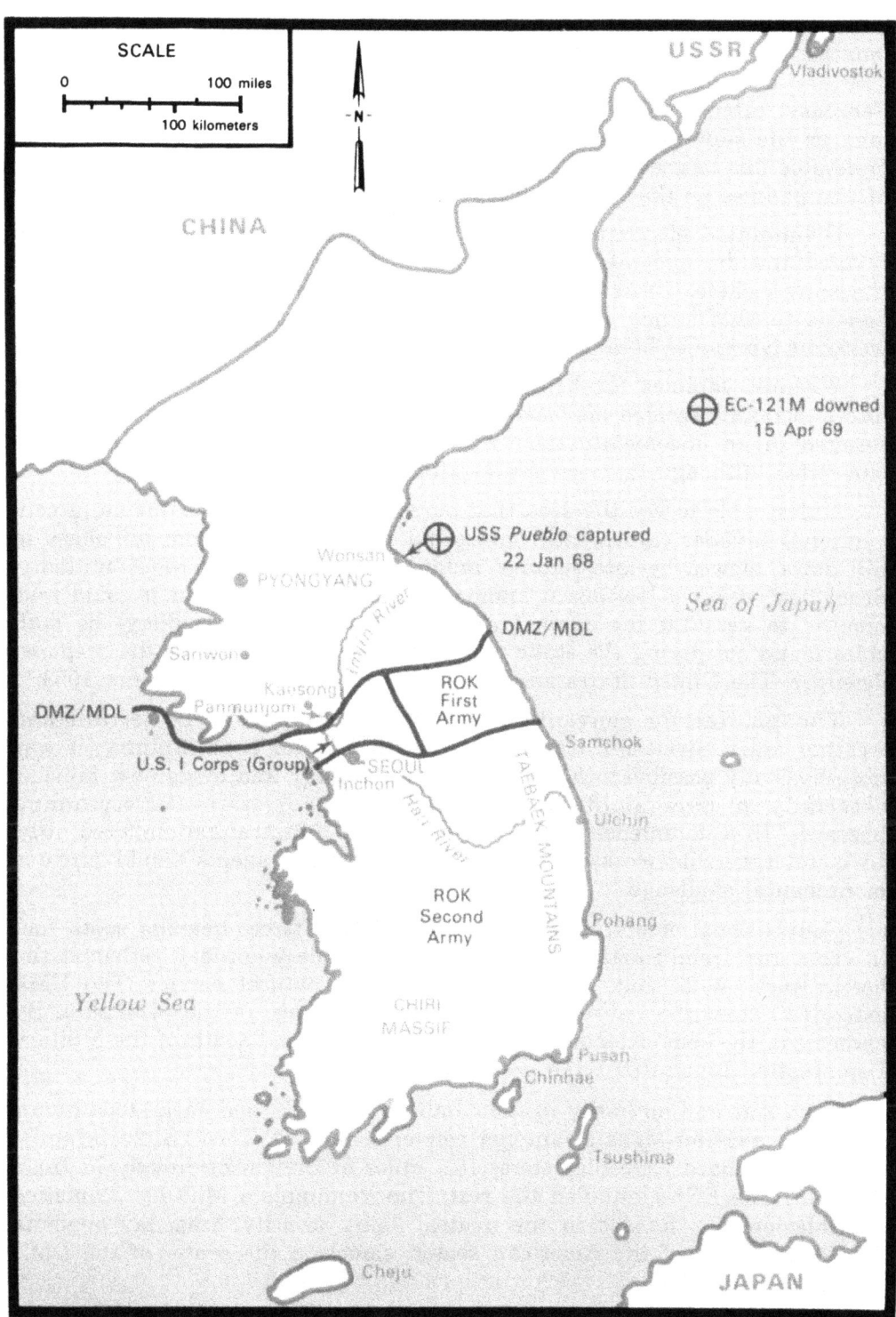

Map 1. Korea, 1966—69

of late summer; frequent storms also made air sorties questionable in these months. In these wet periods, even tracked vehicles could be road bound. The dry periods of late spring (May—June) and midwinter (January—February) offered the best conditions for massed motorized movement. As long as the snows did not get too deep, the cold weather actually could be preferable due to good trafficability on frozen lower slopes and the drainage of rice paddies on the valley floors.

Dismounted elements could move year-round. North Korean agents favored the dry ground, longer nights, and fogs of early autumn—before the snows came. Unlike in the spring, the summer vegetation was still present to shield their movements. September, October, and the first two weeks of November became prime infiltration times.

Without vehicles for heat and shelter, troops on foot—even special forces—usually avoided movement in the bitterly cold Korean winters. This resulted in an unconventional warfare "campaign season" from March to November, although there were exceptions.

Unless able to use the seas that surround the Korean peninsula, a conventional invader enjoys little choice but to grind south from hill mass to hill mass, slowed by late summer mud and deep winter snow. Admittedly, Seoul lies within a few dozen kilometers of North Korea, but it could take months to get that far against any sort of determined soldiery—as both sides found out during the static war of 1951—53. Korea favors the prepared defender. The United States and the ROK had been preparing since 1953.[37]

Though fine for conventional defense, this same ROK terrain and weather aided covert infiltrators. Even with a lot of good infantry, it was not physically possible to block every twisting gully and overgrown hillside, especially on dark nights during blinding thunderstorms or screaming blizzards. In a midintensity war, a few "leakers" (infiltrators) mattered little. In counterguerrilla work, however, stopping skilled agents would prove a monumental challenge.

Conventional or not, most North Korean land forces heading south had to cross the Demilitarized Zone. This man-made boundary reflected the battle lines on 27 July 1953 rather than any natural barrier. The DMZ extended across the entire 242 kilometers (151 miles) of the peninsula. By agreement, the zone extended two kilometers north and south of the Military Demarcation Line (MDL), the precise armistice trace.

Each side had authority in their half of the DMZ, and each stood guard with care, alert for signs of another conventional war. The U.S. 2d Infantry Division defended 29.8 kilometers (18.5 miles of the DMZ) directly in front of Seoul. The ROKs handled the rest. The Panmunjom Military Armistice Commission site, located in the neutral Joint Security Area, lay opposite the western part of the American sector, smack in the center of the DMZ proper (see map 2).

Terrain along the DMZ amounted to a microcosm of the ROK. In the American sector, for example, the maze of hills averaged 500 feet in height.

U.S. and South Korean soldiers guarding a sector of the DMZ under harsh circumstances, 26 August 1967

Two major corridors, the Munsan (western) and Chorwon, converged on Seoul. The Imjin River flowed roughly parallel to the DMZ, just behind the forward U.S. positions. Underbrush, tall grass, and thickets choked the lower slopes of the endless succession of ridgelines.[38]

Aside from the rough natural surroundings, both sides had undertaken improvements in the neutral buffer area. These refinements facilitated early warning of any major attack. A string of observation posts, authorized by the truce, dotted each portion of the DMZ itself. Patrols were also permitted on either side of the MDL. The north prepared minefields and fighting positions just north of the DMZ; to a lesser degree, the U.S.-ROK troops also readied defensive lines just south of their side of the zone.

The armistice allowed no crew-served weapons, armored vehicles, artillery, or fortifications in the zone. Each side could send only 1,000 men into the DMZ at any one time. Once there, these temporarily designated "DMZ police" could patrol as necessary "for the conduct of civil administration and relief" on their side of the MDL. Both sides agreed to refrain from firing weapons across the MDL, overflights of the DMZ, and infiltrations of any type. Joint Observer Teams (UN and Chinese-DPRK) and Neutral

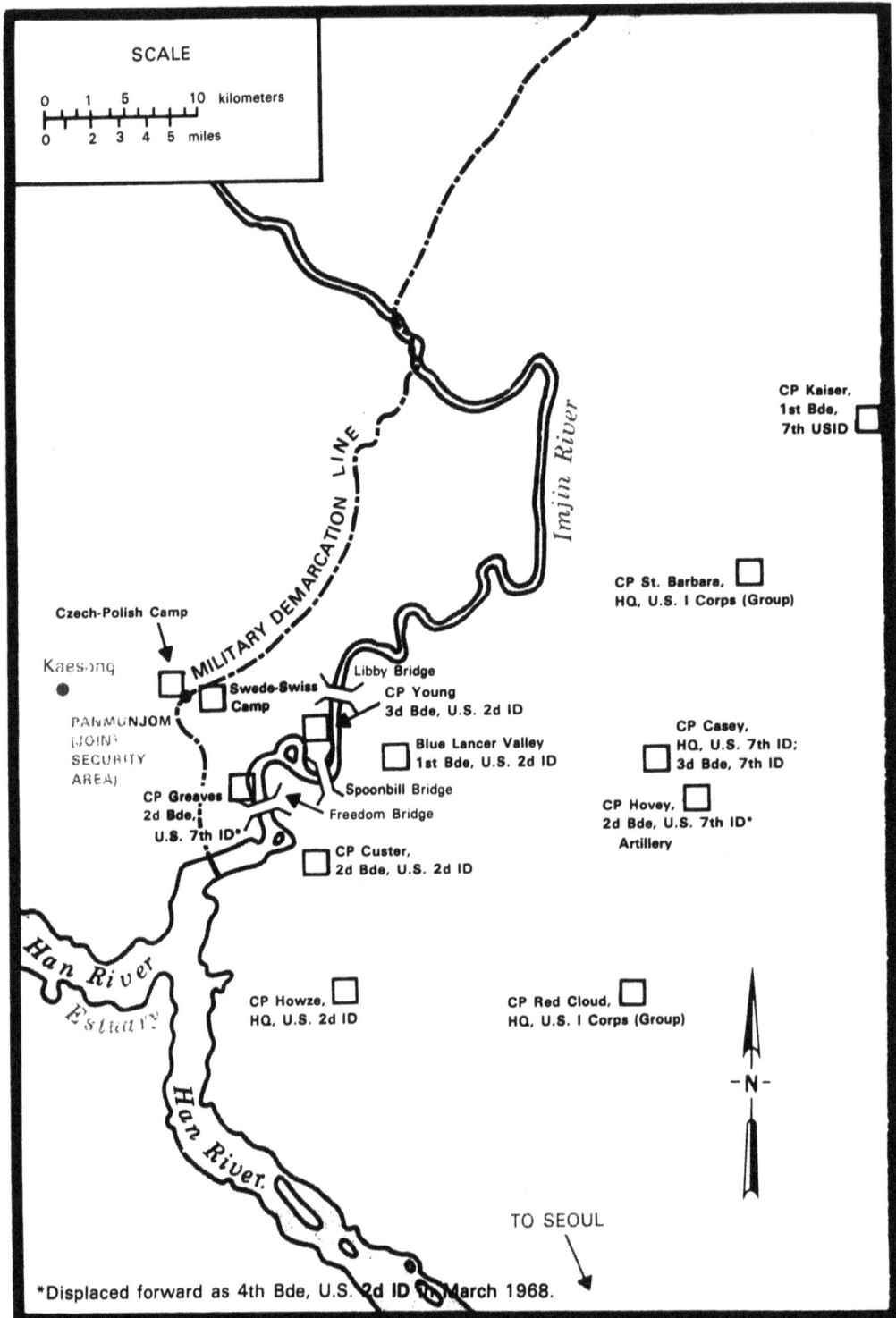

Map 2. The DMZ, U.S. sector, 1966—69

Nations Teams (Swedish, Swiss, Czechs, and Poles) based at Panmunjom supposedly enforced these provisions.

As a practical matter, the North Koreans flouted most of the rules. They fortified their DMZ outposts; introduced machine guns, mortars, and recoilless rifles; and created a special force of permanent DMZ Police well in excess of the numbers allowed. Moreover, they shot at any UN soldier on or near the MDL, including those placing markers in accordance with the armistice.[39] In contrast, United Nations troops generally followed the regulations.

The DMZ constituted the most militarily significant obstacle to land forces moving from north to south. But neither side could cross the DMZ in force without triggering well-prepared defensive schemes. Thanks to their illicit work, the northerners made any movement from south to north incredibly risky. What is more, the KPA could count on secure, well-protected bases of operations for their thrusts south against the more law-abiding UN forces. In time, the allies would emulate their adversaries and become more interested in true counterinfiltration rather than just mere early warning of large-scale attack. But that was not the case in 1966.

Aside from their ground approach, northern forces also could use the seas in attempts to outflank the DMZ. Because the small KPN might carry only a few battalions at most, the threat of a DPRK D day did not exist. Incremental sea infiltration, though, turned out to be another matter. South Korea had to protect almost 6,800 kilometers of irregular, island-strewn seacoast. The narrow coastal plains (five kilometers wide to the east, up to twenty to the west) included most of the important cities, roads, and military facilities—all well within striking distance for seaborne raiders. Conversely, much of the shoreline fronted on remote, sparsely populated wilderness.[40] For agitators determined to reach large segments of the population, establish hidden caches, or create spectacular terrorist incidents, the ROK coastline offered many opportunities.

Along with the topography, the human facets of the South Korean environment deserve a few remarks. Civilian loyalties might determine the fate of the country, particularly if properly manipulated by DPRK guerrilla organizers. Ethnicity, rural sentiments, and the existence of a form of ROK nationalism all bore consideration by both sides.

The Korean population has been described as "one of the most homogeneous in the world."[41] This meant that distinctions between North and South Koreans were largely artificial and that northerners could appeal to a common heritage. On the other hand, most southerners distrusted their North Korean cousins. Traditional regional prejudices—long predating the war—stereotyped northerners as rude and belligerent. The bulk of South Koreans in 1966 vividly remembered the grim events of 1950. Northern aggression only buttressed the old folk beliefs. It hardly helped that Kim Il-sung had called in the hated Chinese and Russians on his behalf.

Besides exploiting ethnic links, North Korea hoped to develop support from rural southerners. Kim Il-sung and his men rightly noted that the

Workmen establishing lights at the chain-link fence aong the DMZ

growth of capitalist industries in the south created social instability—as evidenced by the urban confusion of 1960—61. But Park's coup and subsequent elevation to civil power—in defiance of the Seoul intellectuals and students—convinced the DPRK leadership that agitation among the disgruntled city classes guaranteed little. The majority of South Koreans still lived in farming villages in 1966. As long as the countryside believed in the government and sent its sons into the ROK Army and police, urban insurgents stood little chance of victory.

Could the farmers be subverted? Isolated from the new wealth of the cities, less educated, locally focused, and steeped in superstitious, traditional ways, the Korean farmers looked like a ripe target. They nicely matched the recommended audience for the Maoist ideas in vogue in Kim Il-sung's new military line—or so it seemed.

One crucial difference deserved notice. Since President Rhee's land reform of 1949—50, private farm ownership had become the norm rather than exception; less than 10 percent of the ROK's rural people still worked as tenant laborers by 1966.[42] While not exactly New England yeoman farmers, these Koreans were not penniless peasants. They retained all of the conservatism typical to the countryside, yet in a very real sense, they now owned a piece of the ROK.

Along with southern prejudices and rural attitudes, a degree of discernible ROK nationalism had also arisen. The treaty with Japan, membership in the Asian Pacific Council, rising economic power, and especially the dispatch of ROK forces to aid the mighty United States—all made South Koreans conscious of their country's increasing influence.

North Koreans decried these developments as evidence that the ROK authorities had sold out unification for capitalist treasures. Sometimes it appeared that the ROK had given up Rhee's old goal of bringing the two Koreas together. Yet as President Park put it, ROK economic growth not only brought recognition worldwide, it also provided "a current for national unification," a nebulous phrase that suggested the DPRK could be conquered by southern economic dominance alone.[43] This image of peaceful triumph contrasted sharply with the usual public view of the warlike, crafty northerners.

In sum, the social and economic conditions militated against conventional midintensity conflict. Moreover, the DPRK would need to launch a quick war over ground and under weather that aided the defense, a defense very likely fully alerted by its DMZ trip-wire units. Without a navy, North Korea could only barge south in force and hope for the best. That is, unless it went the low-intensity route.

South Korea offered a guerrilla agitator plenty of access, whether across the overgrown DMZ or along the lengthy, barren coasts. The population in the cities had already shown cracks in its cohesion during Rhee's collapse, and the rural majority might be ripe for propaganda and organization. Environmental factors favored the lone guerrilla, the small special-warfare boat, and the trained terrorist team. The fact that U.S. and ROK troops were not ready for such a campaign only made the terrain benefits that much more useful to northern infiltrators.

## Troops Available

American and South Korean forces on hand in late 1966 formed a strong conventional force. Backed up by the U.S. Fifth Air Force in Japan and Okinawa and the U.S. Seventh Fleet in the western Pacific, these troops deterred overt attacks by North Korea. U.S. capabilities against covert threats existed, but they had yet to be organized into a coherent framework. The UNC land forces positioned one U.S. and nine ROK divisions along the DMZ, backed by another U.S. division and nine more ROK divisions, plus a few separate brigades. Upon mobilization, the ROK Army would be filled out with four ready reserve divisions and six less well-equipped rear-area security divisions.[44]

Provisions for UNC operational control and the ongoing U.S. advisory and assistance program ensured solid cooperation between the allied armies. American headquarters often directed ROK Army units. The I Corps (Group), for example, commanded a mixed force of ROK and U.S. divisions. Now and then, small U.S. forces, typically helicopter or signal units, served under ROK supervision.

Although the most powerful formations on the peninsula, both U.S. Army divisions in Korea suffered from quantitative and qualitative deficiencies (see table 2). Vietnam had priority: Korea would have to fend for itself. U.S. units in Europe drew down too, but they did not fight anyone during this time. U.S. Eighth Army soldiers did, and they started with what they had.

Both American divisions lacked the usual complement of infantry battalions; the U.S. 7th Infantry Division had only one tank battalion instead of the usual two. A pair of mechanized infantry battalions beefed up each division's firepower, partially atoning for the absent battalions. With their reduced establishments, both divisions hobbled along chronically understrength.[45]

Though they had most of their weapons, each division sorely missed the normal complement of helicopters. General Bonesteel recalled: "When I got there on 1 September 1966, there were only four or five Hueys. That was the total number of Hueys in South Korea."[46] Hunting infiltrators in the rough Korean terrain necessitated a lot of trained light infantry or a lot of helicopters to move the infantry on hand; Bonesteel's divisions had neither.

### TABLE 2
### Strength of U.S. Divisions in Korea, 1 January 1968

|  | U.S. 2d Infantry Division | | U.S. 7th Infantry Division | |
| --- | --- | --- | --- | --- |
|  | TOE* | MTOE** | TOE | MTOE |
| Aggregates |  |  |  |  |
| Personnel | 16,810 | 15,057 | 16,810 | 11,300 |
| Helicopters[1] | 88 | 20 | 88 | 20 |
| Tanks | 135 | 135 | 135 | 81 |
| Battalions[2] |  |  |  |  |
| Infantry | 8 | 5 | 8 | 5 |
| Infantry (Mechanized) | 0 | 2 | 0 | 2 |
| Tank | 2 | 2 | 2 | 1 |
| Cavalry | 1 | 1 | 1 | 1 |
| TOTAL | 11 | 10 | 11 | 9 |

*TOE: Table of organization and equipment, a model unit.

**MTOE: Modified table of organization and equipment, theater alterations to ideal unit organizations.

[1]In Korea, divisions substituted elderly, underpowered OH-23 Raven helicopters for modern OH-6A Cayuse and UH-1D Iroquois (Huey) types.

[2]Infantry battalions in Vietnam habitually formed a fourth rifle company; those in Korea retained the traditional three companies.

Sources: United States, Congress, Senate, Committee on Armed Services, *Combat Readiness of United States and South Korean Forces in South Korea*, 90th Cong., 2d sess. (Washington, DC, 7 June 1968), 4—5; United States Department of the Army, Table of Organization and Equipment no. 7 G, *Infantry Division* (Washington, DC: United States Government Printing Office, 31 March 1966), 2, 10, 17, 64, 66, 72; Robert A. Doughty, *The Evolution of US Army Tactical Doctrine, 1946—76*, Leavenworth Papers no. 1 (Fort Leavenworth, KS: Combat Studies Institute, United States Army Command and General Staff College, 1979), 21; and Stanton, *Vietnam Order of Battle*, 47—54, 340—41.

Trimmed numbers did not help, but the uneven quality of U.S. units hurt even more. Firepower might mask these flaws in a big war, but they showed up only too well in small-unit clashes with the skilled North Korean special operators. Old weapons, thirteen-month tours, some poor soldiers, and weak leadership also hampered unit performance. The last problem exacerbated the first three.

Weapons were not first-rate. U.S. troops in Korea did not have the new M-16 automatic rifles, M-48A3 diesel-engine tanks, or UH-1 turbine-powered helicopters. They got by with heavy M-14 semiautomatic rifles and tired M-48A2C gasoline-engine tanks.

They tried to get by with their old, small helicopters, but that did not work. Aside from a handful of UH-1B and UH-1D Hueys, the Americans relied on underpowered, bubble-topped OH-23 Ravens—each able to carry only a pilot and one passenger.[47] Bonesteel pooled the few available Hueys at I Corps (Group), the headquarters that controlled both divisions.

Like their fellow Americans in Vietnam, most U.S. soldiers in Korea served a short tour. With few exceptions, they came and went as individuals, not units. Soldiers remained in country thirteen months (a month longer than Army troops in Vietnam). Bonesteel could and did extend key and essential men up to two more months. A few officers stayed even longer, typically to fill crucial command and staff slots.

The individual rotation policy affected American abilities to function in the demanding Korean environment. On the positive side, every unit had veterans. On the negative side, many American companies seemed like collections of strangers rather than well-honed teams. Each arrival and departure tended to reshuffle everyone to keep key roles covered. Rifle squads rarely maintained the same roster for two weeks in a row. Thus, American units in Korea remained in a state of constant flux, even when not taking casualties.

Troop quality could have been better. Korea received more than its share of the sad "Project 100,000" soldiers—disadvantaged young men inducted into the U.S. Army as sort of an "armed Job Corps." Uneducated, unruly, and unhappy, these people gravitated toward the military equivalent of unskilled labor—the infantry.[48] They demanded extra training time and created numerous disciplinary headaches. Some performed well. Many did not.

Along with a "Project 100,000" soldier, most rifle squads also had a KATUSA (Korean Augmentation to U.S. Army) soldier. This system remained as a holdover from a 1950 program designed to flesh out understrength U.S. units, provide a quick infusion of "local knowledge," and train South Koreans in U.S. techniques.[49] While potentially very useful in counterinsurgency work, KATUSAs presented their U.S. chain of command with a soldier typically weak in his command of English and understanding of modern mechanical technology. Again, the consequent inefficiencies resulted in the loss of valuable tactical training time.

Weak leadership made everything worse. Short tours and the priority on Vietnam meant that veteran officers and sergeants simply were not there. Those that were assigned often represented a conglomerate of inexperience and sloth that might be charitably called "the second string." One brigade commander lamented that "junior leaders lacked the basic skills to take full charge of their men and lead them effectively and aggressively."[50] Why?

Vietnam exerted a powerful influence on professional Army leaders. The centrifugal effects of mounting casualties and brief tours pulled officers and NCOs into Vietnam like water sucked toward a drain. It was not all by force. Many leaders volunteered for Southeast Asia. Good men wanted to be there, not in the perceived Korean backwater. Nobody expected to be part of an "economy of force" mission save the lazy, who were not wanted anyway. As one general commented, "I've known of officers who have chosen retirement rather than come here because they thought it was a dead end."[51]

At the officer level, Bonesteel and his commanders made do with what they had. Often, this meant that senior leaders stretched themselves very thin by closely supervising poor officers or very junior officers. Raw second lieutenants led platoons for a few months, then succeeded to company command. With lieutenant colonels in short supply, majors often commanded battalions for up to a year. Even the U.S. Eighth Army staff seemed full

Soldiers from the U.S. 2d Infantry Division prepare to move out along the DMZ. One soldier (fourth from left) is a KATUSA.

of young lieutenants routinely coming and going rather than the school-trained majors and lieutenant colonels normally authorized.[52]

Sergeants, the backbone of the U.S. Army, were at a real premium. But daily work had to be done, and somebody had to try to take charge. To build up some noncommissioned leadership, the U.S. units resorted to divisional schools. After a few weeks of tactical instruction, the students received their stripes.[53] Such schools produced graduates, but only time could make them real sergeants. This put even more burden on the under-strength, overworked American officer corps.

Though weaker in firepower than the two U.S. divisions, the ROK Army fielded full-strength units. For the ROKs, Vietnam was clearly a secondary task. Defending South Korea stayed the top priority—and very nearly the only priority in times of crisis.

The ROKs did have problems. By and large, they carried weapons two generations behind the new models used in Southeast Asia. For example, they still used semiautomatic Garand M1 rifles—good but dated against a KPA foe armed with automatic AK-47s.[54] The ROKs possessed only a few helicopters.

While the ROKs might have preferred better weapons, few could criticize the quantity and quality of the Korean rank and file. Draftees ordinarily served all thirty-three months of active duty in the same company, allowing almost three times the stability of the U.S. system. American observers rated the ROK line soldiers as "well trained" and praised the "high esprit" in their outfits.[55]

ROK Army officers normally remained in duty positions longer than their American counterparts, although this varied depending upon the individual. ROK Army commanders down to corps level, and occasionally below, benefited from a well-established system of American assistance—the famous Korean Military Advisory Group (KMAG), created in 1949. Beginning in 1964, in a major change of previous policy dating back to the Korean War, the American advisers began to turn over routine training and planning to the ROKs. Bonesteel summarized: "the advisers were no longer telling them when to blow their noses." Not surprisingly, cautious ROK officers did not exactly jump at their new-found freedom—at least at first. They got better, but they were definitely still in transition when their northern foes struck in 1966.

Regardless of KMAG's work, ROK Army leadership certainly had its own way of doing business. While competent and well versed in U.S. Army doctrine, South Korean officers tended to treat American field manuals as prescriptive orders rather than descriptive conceptual approaches. When stumped, they waited for guidance. This did not always come, as Korean officers tended to suppress embarrassing news rather than risk offending their American superiors and advisers. If things went according to plan, the ROK Army excelled. If not, "they didn't know how to operate," as Bonesteel bluntly concluded.[56]

In the air, Bonesteel could count on the American 314th Air Division of a few dozen warplanes and a small but solid ROK Air Force. The U.S. fighter-bombers ensured a nuclear capacity if that became necessary. In addition, the U.S. Fifth Air Force in Japan promised ready reinforcement, but Bonesteel always considered a surprise air attack from the north to be his greatest nightmare.[57] Like the U.S. Army, the U.S. Air Force diverted most of its effort to Vietnam. Thus, the U.S. 314th Air Division and the Fifth Air Force in South Korea often were undermanned.

At sea, Bonesteel had almost no U.S. help beyond a few port units and some Navy and Marine advisers. The sea areas around Korea belonged to an independent command, the U.S. Seventh Fleet, which mainly operated off Vietnam. The ROK Navy, opined U.S. admirals, "could handle the north Korean Navy, which they strongly outgun." The ROKs also had an amphibious capability worth reckoning.[58] But the ROK fleet showed little capability against sea infiltrators—the most likely way in which the KPN would present itself.

The ROK also did not have any special counterguerrilla units or village militia in 1966, despite extensive experience battling partisans in 1950—53. Ad hoc contingents of the ROK Army and Korean National Police had sufficed to meet these disturbances. Unlike the DPRK, the ROK lacked an equivalent of the North Korean Ministry of Internal Affairs. The ROK Army, its Counterintelligence Corps, the National Police (KNP), and the Korean Central Intelligence Agency (KCIA) all pursued infiltrators.[59] But no central directive apparatus existed.

Given advantageous terrain and rough equivalence in numbers, the U.S.-ROK forces stood a good chance against a conventional North Korean attack. With all their nagging troubles, both the U.S. and ROK armies had made quantum improvements since the Korean War. But the enemy would not come that way again, at least not right away, and the U.S.-ROK forces lacked any concerted, systematic means of combating unconventional operations.

## *Time*

American forces in Korea enjoyed an unaccustomed boon, rare in the post-1945 U.S. military experience: regardless of considerable grumbling in the military and among the citizenry, America had chosen to make a long-term military commitment to Korea. The U.S.-ROK 1954 Mutual Defense Treaty "remained in force indefinitely."[60] Of course, a major war in Korea might cause some reevaluation of that open-ended commitment. But America had accepted some DMZ casualties since 1953. As long as casualties stayed at that level, General Bonesteel had all the time he needed.

The South Koreans would not throw in the towel—regardless of the scale or duration of fighting. They definitely were in for as long and as much as it took to overcome any incursions. Any alternative amounted to national extinction.

Typically, one thinks of America constrained by time in war, particularly in a protracted insurgent struggle. Yet in this case, it was Kim Il-sung of North Korea who wanted quick results from his guerrillas. By simply holding on, without cracking and without escalating the conflict, the United States and the Republic of Korea would be victorious. In the Second Korean Conflict, time favored the allies.

---

# Concrete Actions 2

> There is a very definite pattern, and these are not hit and miss tactics.
>
> —an infantry captain,
> U.S. Eighth Army, Korea, 1967

Kim Il-sung's new military line began to take shape as early as the autumn of 1964. Greater numbers of agents attempted to enter the Republic of Korea. Most of these infiltrators came from the propagandists of the Korean Workers' Party Liaison Department and the KPA General Political Bureau. They intended to size up their ROK opponents much like previous intelligence operatives had done. But they also hoped to start laying the groundwork for insurrection.

By October 1966, these stepped-up irregular operations had run afoul of ROK Army patrols and uncooperative southern villagers. ROK regulars suffered almost three dozen fatalities in a series of clashes; some two dozen civilians also died in cross fires and terrorist attacks. The number of DMZ incidents climbed noticeably in the ROK sectors. Hostile probes also increased along South Korea's coastlines. ROK sailors flushed a KPN midget submarine in the Imjin River estuary, chased North Korean spy boats among the east coast shallows, and exchanged gunfire with pugnacious KPN patrol craft.[1]

Throughout these two tense years, the American sector remained ominously quiet. It almost appeared that, whatever their motives, the Korean Communists had chosen to avoid U.S. units. That comforting situation was about to change.

## A Call to Arms

The scale and intensity of unconventional warfare had grown since the December 1962 proclamation of a new military line, yet these efforts had not really had much impact on the ROK. The DPRK operations lacked focus and hence showed few measurable results.

Kim Il-sung decided to change that. In a lengthy speech to the Second Korean Workers' Party (KWP) Conference on 5 October, the northern premier outlined his refurbished campaign plan.[2] He stated his goal,

33

explained a sequence of events to bring about that goal, and described the means to be employed (see figure 4). Kim left no doubt as to his priority: "Comrades," he said, "the greatest national task confronting the KWP and the Korean people at the present stage is to accomplish the country's unification and the victory of the revolution on a nationwide scale."

---

Strategic objective: Unification of Korea under the DPRK.

Operational objectives (in sequence):
- Create military-industrial base for revolution in DPRK.
- Neutralize United States in Korea; break U.S.-ROK alliance.
- Subvert/liberate ROK.

Means: Combination of methods (conventional/unconventional).

Sources: Compiled from Kim Il-song, "The International Situation and Problems of the World Communist Movement," in his *Revolution and Socialist Construction in Korea* (New York: International Publishers, 1971), 113—15; and Bermudez, *North Korean Special Forces*, 30.

---

Figure 4. DPRK campaign plan (new military line), announced 5—12 October 1966

Even as early as 1963, Communist inflitrators directed their violence on U.S. and ROK troops, as witnessed by this ambushed jeep

How would this be done? Kim Il-sung laid out a three-phase course of action. First, he exhorted his party faithful to "push ahead vigorously with the revolution" in the north, thereby building "a powerful base for revolution." While Kim judged this work to be well advanced, he insisted upon "acceleration" of the ongoing military and industrial modernization. Second, the Communist chief believed that in order to destroy the "puppet government" in Seoul, he had to neutralize its puppet master. Why? Because according to Kim, "the US occupation and its colonial rule over South Korea is the root cause of all misfortunes and sufferings the South Korean people are undergoing and the main obstacle to unification of our country." Such ranting against Yankee "imperialism" was hardly novel. Kim's prescription, however, struck a new chord that went beyond simple rhetoric. "It is also wrong merely to shout against US imperialism without taking concrete actions to stop its aggression," he said. Unable to defeat America outright, Kim hoped to strain and break its ties to the Republic of Korea.

The time to split the two looked ripe. The United States had many interests aside from Korea, most obviously the war in Vietnam. The United States should wish to avoid another land war in Asia. Kim wanted to increase the price of the United States staying in Korea beyond what it would be willing to pay. He could use bloody, direct attacks or, through provocations, induce the ROKs to demand a much heavier U.S. commitment. Either way, the Americans might lose heart. Kim argued thusly: "In the present situation the US imperialist should be dealt blows and their forces dispersed to the maximum in all parts of the world and on every front—in Asia and Europe, Africa and Latin America, and in all countries, big and small. They should be bound hand and foot everywhere they set foot so that they may not act arbitrarily."

Once America began to doubt itself or relinquish its role in Korea, then the DPRK could shift to phase three: the incitement of a broad-based insurgency designed to topple the Park government. This would be marked by "a rapid expansion of the revolutionary forces and an acceleration of the democratic revolution for national liberation in every way." Kim implied that the preparations for phase three would coincide with the phase two struggle against United States forces in Korea. Whether the final takeover would come by ground invasion or popular revolution remained unresolved and depended upon the success of the insurgents.

Either way, the DPRK must be ready. Having announced his aim and discussed his concept of operations, the northern leader threw the full weight of his state's resources behind the undertaking. He directed the use of "a combination of methods involving all kinds of struggle in correspondence to the objective and subjective situations: political struggle and economic struggle, violent struggle and nonviolent struggle, and legal and illegal struggle." By stressing "methods" rather than types of forces, Kim sent an important message to his own armed services. Conventional or unconventional, all North Korean components would contribute.

The DPRK premier did not specify a timetable for his campaign, but he did stress that "unification of the fatherland is the supreme national task of our people and an urgent question which brooks no further delay."[3] The public record contains nothing more definite. Kim Il-sung, however, implied a possible completion date in another statement at the same party conference. He pointedly extended the fulfillment of the Seven Year Plan from October 1967 until October 1970.[4] The course of later developments seems to confirm this possible schedule. In any event, Kim left no doubt that he expected swift progress.

Kim backed up his words with deeds. He fired the leaders of the KWP Liaison Department, its subordinate Guerrilla Guidance Section, and the associated KPA Propaganda and Instigation Bureau. These unfortunates went off to penal camps. They had been judged too disorganized, too slow, and altogether too soft.

In their stead, Kim turned to military hard-liners who promised quick, dramatic results. To underscore this change of policy, he promoted a group of generals drawn mainly from his old Kapsan band, veterans of the guerrilla fight against Japan from 1936—45. Six of eleven new Politburo members came from this military faction.

The North Korean dictator also emphasized a new primacy for the KPA Reconnaissance Bureau in running unconventional missions. Party propagandists and activists took backseats to army terrorists and commandos. The KPA commenced a crash program to create elite special warfare contingents, which eventually became famous as the all-officer 124th and 283d Army Units. But these superb outfits would not be ready until 1968.[5] Until then, the Reconnaissance Bureau had to use what it had and could borrow, to include party cadres, security formations, and regular military units. Spurred by their supreme leader's vision and pressed by their newly promoted generals, North Korean special operators went to work. This time, as Kim Il-sung warned, the unwitting Americans were "target No. 1."[6]

## First Blood

President Lyndon B. Johnson could not have chosen a worse time to visit Seoul. General Bonesteel had been in command only about two months. He spent most of that time trying to separate fact from fiction along the DMZ. In the meantime, deadly incidents and rumors of future incidents proliferated. The ROK First Army, for instance, reported numerous skirmishes on its eastern part of the DMZ. The UNC took no action beyond ordering defensive precautions. But the ROKs had put up with enough. Late in October, frustrated South Koreans conducted a cross-border retaliatory raid without seeking Bonesteel's approval. As a result, American KMAG advisers argued with their ROK counterparts. The U.S. officers wanted to prevent another armistice violation; Korean officers countered that the Americans paid too little attention to ROK casualties. Tempers flared. Meanwhile, probably tipped off by their own intelligence, the North Koreans struck again and again in the ROK Army areas, fanning dissension between the allies.

Alarmed by the steady increase in violent incidents, the UNC raised the alert status of all forces in the weeks prior to Johnson's arrival. Bonesteel ordered especially stringent measures in the combined U.S.-ROK I Corps (Group)—the "shield of Seoul"—which defended the western segment of the DMZ. The U.S. 2d Infantry Division braced for trouble along the DMZ.[7] More patrols went out, and each night, tanks rolled forward to play their brilliant xenon searchlights across suspected infiltration lanes.

Unfazed by the rising wave of North Korean belligerence, President Johnson came to Korea on 31 October, trailed by a bustling entourage of more than 500 people. He met with President Park, U.S. Ambassador Winthrop G. Brown, General Bonesteel, and American troops at Camp Stanley—all in a frenzied forty-four hours.[8] United Nations Command forces remained ready, but the DPRK made no move against Johnson.

Instead, the North Koreans took action against Johnson's men. In the predawn darkness on 2 November, while the American president slept near Seoul under heavy guard, a KPA squad tracked an eight-man patrol from Company A, 1-23 Infantry. The northerners, probably from the 17th Foot Reconnaissance Brigade, paralleled the oblivious American soldiers. Once the U.S. element reached a point about a kilometer south of the DMZ

President Lyndon B. Johnson

proper, the North Koreans estimated that the Americans had relaxed their vigilance. The Communist soldiers swung in ahead of the plodding American file, assumed hasty ambush positions, and engaged the Americans with hand grenades and submachine guns.

The U.S. squad disintegrated under a hail of bullets and grenade fragments. Despite later wishful stories of heroics, six Americans and a KATUSA went down almost instantly. A seventh American survived by playing dead. The KPA troops pumped a few more bursts into some of the corpses, plunged in a bayonet here and there, and disappeared into the

South Koreans welcoming President Lyndon Johnson to Korea

night. One northerner might have been wounded in the one-sided fight. The sole American survivor ran for his life as soon as the attackers pulled out.

Almost simultaneously, another KPA squad surprised a patrol in ROK First Army. Two South Koreans died before the northerners withdrew.[9] That ended the shooting, but it was enough for one night. The twin strikes had been well timed, well executed, and very effective.

If the North Koreans expected to make a political statement by these terrorist attacks, they must have been gratified by the next day's news headlines in the United States. The nearby presidential press corps, no doubt bored by the routine diplomatic meetings and photo opportunities, pounced on the bloody story of the lost U.S. patrol (almost wholly ignoring the coincident ROK Army losses, not to mention previous southern battle deaths). For one day, Korea displaced Vietnam from the front pages of American newspapers.[10] Then Johnson left for home and interest waned.

Bonesteel's interest did not subside, nor did that of his men and his ROK allies. The general observed that these "vicious, provocative raids" looked "considerably different from actions in previous years." Now, KPA "hunter-killer" squads sought Americans.[11] But why? And what should be done about it?

## Bonesteel's Assessment

The general took it upon himself to address the problem. Had he been less sure of his abilities, he might have turned to Ambassador Brown and the rest of the "country team" in Korea. In compliance with the Mutual Defense Assistance Act of 1949, the ambassador coordinated the diverse U.S. organizations in Korea. He directed his own foreign service personnel and supervised the local offices of the Central Intelligence Agency, Agency for International Development, and U.S. Information Service. Anywhere else, Brown would have also controlled the activities of the U.S. military advisers in country, although this was not the case in Korea thanks to the persistence of the wartime military command structure.

With its round table of competing bureaucracies chaired by a diplomat, the country team model amounted to leadership by committee. It promised little, however, in the face of the new northern aggression. In this instance (because he could), Bonesteel chose to avoid the entire country team mess.

Unlike Westmoreland in Vietnam, Bonesteel did not have to report to the ambassador with regard to operational matters. Under his hat as commander in chief of UNC, he dealt directly with the secretary of defense and, by extension, the president. His military status also helped him exert influence on retired General Park Chung Hee and his administration of former ROK Army men; after all, Bonesteel wielded operational control of Park's South Korean military. While President Johnson required that Bonesteel and his ambassador maintain "close relations," the general interpreted this requirement liberally. While he coordinated closely with

Ambassador Brown, an old acquaintance, Bonesteel made his own decisions.[12]

Thanks to his acute analytical powers, Bonesteel went beyond the simple recognition that something unprecedented had occurred. By taking the time to ask the right questions rather than rushing to act or blithely resorting to usual responses, Bonesteel acknowledged the complexities of his situation. He determined to find out why things had changed before ordering countermeasures. Characteristically, he initiated measures himself and ensured that his subordinates worked quickly once he issued his guidance.

Bonesteel asked his intelligence officers for their judgments. "So," he recalled, "I got the G-2 people together, all of them, and learned not too damned much about what had been going on up north." The intelligence staff regurgitated hard data on KPA organizations, weapons, training, locations, and recent DMZ activities. They also listed countless political, economic, and social indicators. But none of the staff officers could find any coherent pattern in the mass of detail.

Bonesteel could and did. He immersed himself in the issue in the days following the 2 November attacks. Determined to understand the larger purposes of the enemy's scheme, he ignored the mountain of sightings and radio interceptions and went to the only source that really mattered: "I personally read all the speeches that Kim Il-sung made the previous two years," he said, "those that were overt and some that were semi-classified that we had obtained in some way or another. This was pretty interesting because he had developed a regular *Mein Kampf*."

Bonesteel's exhaustive research allowed him to trace the genesis and content of Kim's October 1966 campaign plan. "He laid out his strategy for the coming years," explained Bonesteel; "Reading it in the communist dialectic lexicon, it was pretty plain what they were going to do or at least try to do."[13] Thus, within days of the DPRK double strike, Bonesteel accurately discerned Kim Il-sung's intentions, to include the probable sequence of major operational phases.[14] But how could the Communists be stopped without starting a midintensity war?

Bonesteel had his own ideas, but he also had time. The days after 2 November were devoid of action as winter blew in throughout Korea. With the parameters of the threat now clear, Bonesteel wanted to make use of this lull to bring in other minds and other perspectives and to develop solutions.

As early as 6 November, the general formed his brightest staff men into a Special Working Group. Although the group enjoyed a broad charter to scrutinize the entire Korean situation, Bonesteel did not just turn them loose. The general gave specific guidance and suggestions and checked frequently on the group's progress. To a great extent, the group's findings and recommendations simply implemented Bonesteel's own original thinking. There would be other studies, commanders' calls, visits, and fact-finding conferences to study the Korean situation, most notably the definitive Counterinfiltration-Guerrilla Concept Requirements Plan of late 1967. Even so, the Special Working Group's report gave the first clear explanation of Bonesteel's vision of how to fight and win this unexpected Second Korean Conflict.

Bonesteel placed only one ironclad constraint on his Special Working Group: he insisted on Korean participation in planning its country's defense. The general made it clear to his key subordinates that he "wanted to put the responsibility on the ROKs."[15] Given the rudimentary Korean representation in the American-dominated higher headquarters, this was a bold move. From a counterinsurgency perspective, it proved essential.

## *The Doctrinal Void*

American and Korean officers searching for countermeasures to the new KPA threat relied on the same body of printed and schooled doctrine. Unfortunately, that material described conventional solutions inappropriate to unconventional problems. U.S. Army doctrine did not really allow for the nature of the war under way in Korea and thus could only offer a few half-baked practical hints.

Army doctrine at that time proposed a spectrum of conflict roughly similar to that currently envisioned—but one described and analyzed hazily at the lower end of the continuum. A command of Bonesteel's size would refer to FM 100-15, *Field Service Regulations Larger Units* (corps to theater), for doctrinal guidance. The 1966 edition identified the extremes of the spectrum as cold war and general war ("unrestricted application of military force," i.e., nuclear combat), with limited war in the gray area between.

Korea in 1966 certainly fell short of general war. Was it a cold war or a limited war? The manual's authors defined cold war this way: "a state of international tension wherein political, economic, technological, sociological, psychological, paramilitary, and military measures, short of overt armed conflict involving regular military forces, are employed to achieve national objectives." That sounded like Korea, except there, regular forces had joined the fray on both sides, and there had been overt armed conflict, with more impending.

The Army described limited war as an "overt engagement" for limited ends with limited means. These examples were provided: "local aggression," "conventional war," and "limited nuclear war."[16] Did Korea constitute "local aggression," whatever that meant? There had certainly been overt engagement.

This theoretical ambiguity characterized most of the U.S. Army doctrine of that period. Contemporary doctrine visualizes a more fully developed view of low-intensity conflict under the broad categories of peacekeeping,

A U.S. Army freight train falls victim to saboteurs north of Seoul, Korea, 13 September 1967

---

### Low-Intensity Conflict (Cold War): U.S.-ROK Versus DPRK

Peacekeeping:

- U.S. membership in Military Armistice Commission, Panmunjom.
- U.S.-ROK DMZ duties under the Korean Armistice Agreement of 27 July 1953.

Combating Terrorism:

- U.S.-ROK DMZ and coast anti-infiltration operations.
- ROK police/military counterterrorist operations.
- U.S.-ROK military antiterrorism operations.

Counterinsurgency:

- U.S.-ROK intelligence operations.
- U.S.-ROK combined joint-service exercises.
- U.S.-ROK civil-military infrastructure development.
- U.S.-ROK humanitarian and civic assistance (U.S. Eighth Army Cold War Program).
- U.S.-ROK logistics operations.
- ROK populace and resources control operations.
- U.S.-ROK DMZ coast anti-infiltration operations.

Contingencies:

- U.S. shows of force (USS *Pueblo*, EC-121M incidents).

### Midintensity Conflict (Limited War): U.S.-ROK versus DPRK (with PRC*/USSR Support)

U.S.-ROK conventional defense of the Republic of Korea.

### High-Intensity Conflict (General War): U.S.-ROK versus DPRK and/or PRC and/or USSR

U.S.-ROK nuclear defense of the Republic of Korea.

U.S.-nuclear strikes on DPRK and/or PRC and/or USSR.

*People's Republic of China

---

Figure 5. The spectrum of conflict in Korea, 1966—69

combating terrorism, counterinsurgency, and contingencies.[17] Each of these types of operations occurred during the Second Korean Conflict (see figure 5).

Today, U.S. Army field manuals (still too few, but some) explain how to approach such operations. But doctrinal writers of the 1960s, because they never really came to grips with the distinctive natures of limited versus cold wars, mainly avoided the whole mess. A reader poring over FM 100-15 would find no further references to cold or limited wars beyond the definitions noted above. If he dug around, a diligent man might unearth a single, bland paragraph on counterinsurgency or a short paragraph on unconventional warfare that explained the utility of pro-American partisans in enemy rear areas.[18] The rest of the manual discussed what today would be called midintensity conflict. Basically, FM 100-15, like its many relatives, told soldiers how to refight World War II.

If one delved into the lower echelon division manual, FM 61-100 (1965 edition), one would find some practical, generic advice about small wars. The divisional doctrine devoted almost two whole pages to "Cold War Situations." It was a mixed bag, but at least it was something.

The doctrine writers had given the issue some thought. They warned of the need to consider political implications and restrictions on tactical methods and missions and warned a cold war commander to expect non-military, "unpredictable factors" to influence his traditional battlefield ways. In order to meet these demanding situations, the manual mentioned useful training subjects for a cold war force: civil-military relations, local language and customs, rules of engagement, patrolling, and counterinfiltration. Rotation of committed units was suggested to allow continued training of troops on these difficult subjects. The eventual UNC approach took heed of this information.

The rest of the material consisted of well-meaning drivel. One paragraph called infantry battalions "well suited for the control of mobs and for the suppression of riots and civil disorders." Another noted that armored cavalry and tanks could be "effective in quelling riots." Aviation might serve for reconnaissance, supply, liaison, and loudspeaker work; air assaults received little consideration. A concluding paragraph recommended the use of riot control chemicals as necessary. To read this, one might get the impression that cold war operations equaled urban riot suppression.

The divisional doctrine had two other subjects of interest, under separate headings. A half-page commentary on "counterinsurgency" called the division "particularly well suited" to such missions—although no particular proof supported this claim. In the "unconventional warfare" section, the authors offered a contrast to illustrate their points about guerrilla fighting. Whereas Special Forces (Green Berets) work in the enemy rear, "the conventional forces are most generally concerned with guerrilla warfare" in friendly areas.[19] There was no discussion of how to conduct such operations, leading to the logical conclusion that they were to be handled in traditional ways by conventional units "well suited" to such actions.

With little to gain from the most common doctrinal sources, what of the more specialized manuals? The U.S. Army's "31-series" purported to address small wars, but by the 1960s, these works generally offered guidance written by and for Special Forces. While theoretically interesting, they all presumed the availability of Special Forces elements in theater. Bonesteel had no Green Berets in Korea. He did, however, have a low-intensity conflict.

Only one "31-series" manual directly addressed conventional forces in unconventional wars: FM 31-16, *Counterguerrilla Operations*. This work encouraged the U.S. commander to employ his superior mobility and firepower to find, fix, fight, and finish guerrillas. Local forces were only useful as trackers, interpreters, and in some static security jobs. Killing guerrillas equaled victory. Standard U.S. Army tactics and powerful U.S. Army units would suffice for that. Since American forces were to carry the brunt of the fight to kill guerrillas, it made sense that they should be used as mobile reserves, not tied down in defense of fixed locations, such as at borders.

The authors of FM 31-16 recommended that frontier security operations "be conducted by indigenous forces to economize on the available (U.S.) military combat power which can be better utilized against the guerrilla force." To handle a trace like the DMZ against an unconventional threat, FM 31-16 would turn the whole thing over to the South Koreans in order to free up stronger U.S. units to pounce on guerrillas in the interior.[20] That concept, described in four pages, was about the only printed U.S. Army doctrine that specifically applied to Bonesteel's predicament in Korea. And it was wrong.

Obviously, perfect hindsight enables one to find much fault with U.S. Army LIC doctrine of the 1960s. But at the time, most of it had yet to be called into question—nor would it be until much later, well after the end of the Vietnam War.[21] Nothing written or taught as U.S. Army doctrine discussed peacekeeping, actions against terrorists, or contingency operations under any heading, even though U.S. forces, including those in Korea, did such missions throughout the 1960s. Doctrinal authors of that era also appeared blissfully unaware of the political dangers of a "go it alone" Americanized approach to small wars.

So not much applicable doctrine existed, and what did might well be considered counterproductive. Given that Bonesteel's U.S. and ROK forces had been steeped in this inadequate doctrine, two alternatives existed. First, the United Nations Command could fight a conventional war against the North Korean infiltrators, modifying standard U.S. Army tactics as necessary to adjust to local conditions. This reflected the choice eventually adopted in Vietnam, where, under this approach, General Westmoreland best expressed the preferred means for defeating insurgents and intruders: "Firepower."[22] Of course, in Korea, that probably meant a major war—and hence failure to achieve one of Bonesteel's principal strategic objectives. With war raging in Vietnam, Bonesteel knew that he had to stop the DPRK in the low-intensity arena—not escalate to the midintensity realm. One Asian war was enough. "I was trying to maintain the peace," he said, "so we wouldn't have to fight another one in Korea."[23]

A second path beckoned. It would involve junking the approved doctrinal framework and inventing unique tactics suited to Korea. Although appealing to Bonesteel's unorthodox streak, this course of action entailed a huge risk. Could the Americans and ROKs, trained for conventional combat, play their required parts in such an effort? True, the general could retrain his own U.S. Army units, subject to the debilitations of inadequate strength and short tours. The real challenges involved dealing with the U.S. Air Force, the U.S. Navy, the U.S. Marines, and especially the ROKs, who enshrined U.S. doctrine as near holy writ. Bonesteel did not control their internal structures, training, or doctrine—save by whatever suasion he could milk from his powers of operational control.

Faced with a doctrinal void and the desire to keep things at a low intensity, Bonesteel trusted his instincts. He cut the umbilical cord. The United Nations Command began to invent its own doctrine to meet its needs. "So," recounted Bonesteel, "we developed these tactics and efforts to get ahead, especially in the DMZ, and I was looking for any kind of idea."[24]

Bonesteel's Special Working Group issued a preliminary report in January 1967. By February, the UNC had started to implement the key recommendations. Based on this study and his personal investigations, Bonesteel recognized that his troops had to conduct three types of operations to beat back the North Korean surge. The first involved "developing a guard against infiltration across the DMZ." The second comprised a similar naval effort along the seacoasts. The third type of operation conceived of counterguerrilla operations in the interior—"an entirely different concept" from the first two tasks.[25] All three types of operations had to be accomplished without jeopardizing the conventional defense of the ROK.

## Anti-Infiltration: The DMZ

Of the three tasks, the land anti-infiltration role most resembled a conventional mission. A manual prepared from the U.S. Eighth Army experience of the late 1960s said: "Border security/anti-infiltration operations follow all the normal doctrinal principles found in the traditional concepts of defense."[26] If a force knew how to conduct an area defense, it could guard the DMZ against both conventional and unconventional threats.

In light of the real dangers of a northern invasion, it only made sense to employ the bulk of the conventionally trained U.S.-ROK forces doing the sorts of things that they would do in a midintensity war. They would not necessarily maintain those skills chasing guerrillas through the hinterlands of South Korea. Bonesteel explained that "the front-line US and ROK divisions are responsible for both the DMZ security mission and the defense mission."[27]

That sounded like the same old approach along the DMZ, and in a sense, it was. There was nothing inherently wrong in *what* the UNC forces were doing; *how* they were doing it created the trouble. Traditional doctrine alone guaranteed more casualties at the hands of KPA elite forces.

Bonesteel could not sit back and let his subordinates resolve these issues. American officers already had their hands full simply running their understrength, underofficered units. The Koreans, for their part, equated most kinds of improvisation to disobedience. With Kim Il-sung's special forces promising a rapid expansion of the campaign in the spring, Bonesteel needed a comprehensive approach, not just a spotty amalgam of random experimentation. After soliciting other views, Bonesteel decided how to fight on the DMZ. As part of his plan, he directed and, more often, encouraged and disseminated others' good ideas. His most important initiatives affected tactics along the DMZ, but he made sure to enhance these new procedures by looser rules of engagement and an integrated DMZ rotation and training plan.

Bonesteel addressed anti-infiltration tactics that detected, delayed, and neutralized intruders.[28] Though fairly capable at neutralization, both the Americans and the South Koreans needed work at detecting and delaying infiltrators. Prior to 1967, most detection occurred by chance, and delay was bought by bloody meeting engagements. Throughout 1967, the UNC evolved a four-layer defense against infiltration. Not only did the defense have to work, but it had to comply with the armistice agreement and do so without draining troops needed for ground defense against conventional invasion. The UNC tested its concepts in the U.S. 2d Infantry Division and the ROK 21st Infantry Division. In a bureaucratic maneuver worthy of the experienced Washington insider that he was, Bonesteel cajoled the U.S. Army Combat Developments Command into giving him some $30 million to create a "DMZ/Barrier testbed" based on his two experimental divisions.[29] In these two divisions, and eventually across the peninsula, four anti-infiltration tiers fell into place. Patrols in the DMZ; guard posts in the DMZ; a new barrier defense system; and new, mobile quick-reaction forces cooperated to find infiltrators, fix them, and destroy them (see figure 6).[30]

Patrols had been going out into the DMZ since the armistice, but for the Americans, these had degenerated into rather pro forma affairs in the long, dull decade after 1953. The 2 November ambush changed that: "The days are gone," mused a U.S. sergeant, "when you could ride out to the DMZ with just a driver, wearing a soft cap."[31] By mid-1967, U.S. patrolling became a very serious business. An American colonel explained that these patrols endeavored "by their presence to deny the area to the north Koreans and to search for signs of enemy activity, hiding places, and infiltration routes."

Squads and platoons patrolled, sometimes as units, sometimes as ad hoc formations. Armistice rules prevented use of machine guns and recoilless rifles. Routes wove in front of, behind, and between the string of guard posts planted in the allied half of the DMZ. Typically, each company had one patrol out at all times, with more after dark and during periods of tension. Patrols tended to go out for twenty-four hours, reconnoitering by day and establishing ambushes at night. Compositions, routes, and timings changed in attempts to confuse the KPA.

Patrolling received command emphasis, but U.S. units never achieved the proficiency of their ROK allies, let alone that of the stealthy North Korean recon troops. A brigade commander conceded that U.S. units "took the most casualties while on patrol."[32] Some of these losses could be attributed to skilled enemies, but many U.S. deaths and wounds arose from inexperienced, inept, or inattentive leadership. Concerned senior commanders tried to reach down and provide the leadership absent from U.S. units. One

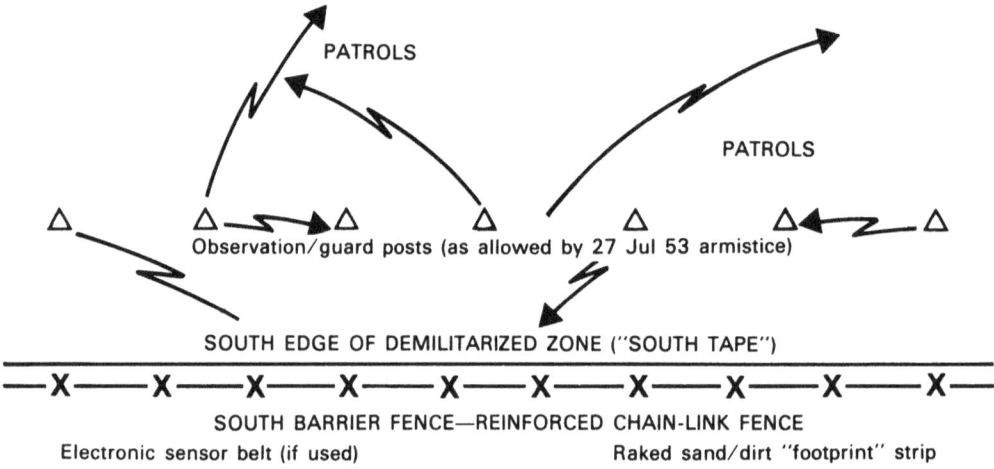

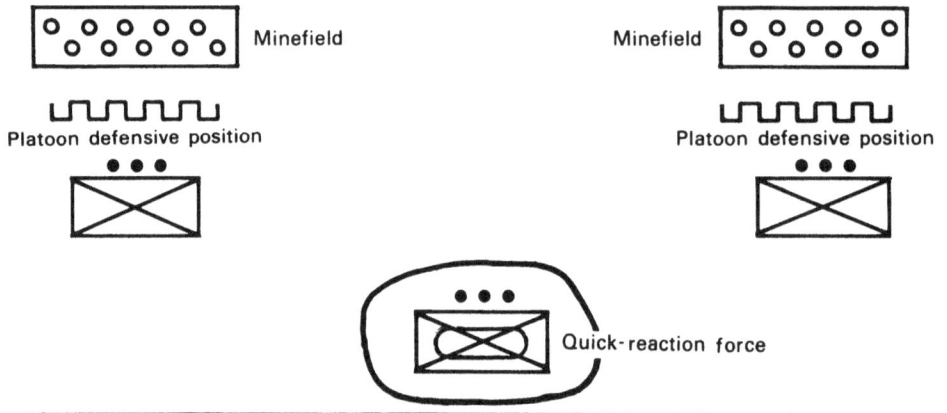

Figure 6. UNC anti-infiltration dispositions (idealized example)

brigade commander required an officer from each company to be on patrol in the DMZ at all times and supplemented this order with "frequent officers' calls, continuous supervision, on-the-spot corrections, and some wholesale butt-chewings."[33] Unnecessary casualties occurred anyway, right down to the end. Bonesteel acknowledged this sloppy U.S. patrolling by caustically granting that "the best counterinfiltration devices were the eyes, ears, and brains of the GI, if you could keep him awake."[34]

The ROKs took casualties, too, despite their better discipline. Proportionate to their strength, though—and even with their many other roles—the ROK Army maintained a lower casualty rate than the American troops.³⁵ The U.S. forces' proximity to Seoul and the main infiltration routes accounted for part of this. On the whole, though, the ROK Army's more cohesive and rigorously trained units patrolled more effectively than their American allies. Did all of these patrols catch many North Koreans? Statistically speaking, they did not. But their constant presence, like policemen on neighborhood beats, complicated and delayed KPA intrusion plans.

In a similar way, the small squad and platoon guard posts in the Demilitarized Zone served as static surveillance sites and bases of fire for beleaguered patrols. Americans stretched the armistice provisions by sandbagging and entrenching these positions. Despite armistice prohibitions against such weapons in the zone, troops often kept machine guns and recoilless rifles hidden but ready for use if needed.³⁶

U.S. units rotated through these posts for stretches of seven to ten days. Except during relatively rare, direct KPA attacks, the troops followed a fairly standard routine. During the day, soldiers on guard post duty rested, trained on small-unit tactics, and rebuilt or extended their field fortifications. At night, they came to full alert. Thanks to Bonesteel's $30 million windfall, the posts often had night-vision devices to watch the DMZ. Hand flares and searchlights also contributed to visibility.

As with patrols, the ROKs played the outpost game better than the Americans. Some U.S. soldiers, said one officer, treated the guard posts as rest areas. Some did not wash or maintain equipment unless closely supervised. Inspections revealed "dirty, bent, and generally unserviceable" ammunition. Part of this resulted from primitive conditions in the newer bunker complexes, especially during the brutal winter. Mostly, though, it was another symptom of weak junior leadership.³⁷

To support the guard posts, Bonesteel, employing his engineering skills, introduced a new barrier defense system incorporating common backyard chain-link fence. The barrier defense system ran along the south trace of the DMZ. Nagging armistice regulations did not apply here, so the UNC could turn its full panoply of assets to the problems of detecting, delaying, and neutralizing infiltrators.

The system centered around a chain-link fence, ten feet tall, topped by triple strands of concertina wire and reinforced by interwoven saplings and steel engineer pickets. A narrow, raked-sand path paralleled the fence on the allied side to highlight footprints. Just past the sand strip lay a 120-meter-wide kill zone cleared with plows, chain saws, axes, and chemical defoliants. In that area, mines and tanglefoot wire fronted a line of conventional defensive positions. From there, defenders used a final protective line of interlocking machine guns and on-call mortar and artillery concentrations to dominate the kill zone. Observation towers stood at intervals along the trace to permit clear view of the open areas. Local patrols checked the fence line and covered dead ground between positions.

It took a combined U.S.-Korean engineer force about two months to finish the test fence in the American sector. Along with the fence, engineers laid mines, built roads to allow quick movements laterally and forward, and cleared dozens of helicopter landing zones. Similar efforts went on in front of the ROK 21st Infantry Division.[38]

Due to his agreement with Combat Developments Command, Bonesteel required his test units to try out a veritable toy store of futuristic Starlight Scope night-vision devices, helicopter-mounted "people sniffers," electrical fence proposals, and unattended ground sensors. It was, after all, the heyday of the "McNamara Line" in Vietnam and the supposed advent of the electronic battlefield. The night illuminating devices proved very useful, and one model of electrical fence functioned well, although it cost too much for widespread use.

The sensors posed special problems. Various types detected seismic vibrations, ground pressure changes, body odors, magnetic disturbances, infrared sources, and acoustic disruptions. Unfortunately, rain, wind, passing trucks, and wandering animals tripped the sensors so often that their indications proved meaningless. Moreover, soldiers detested emplacing, guarding, and maintaining the temperamental things. Scientists brought model after model for evaluation, but none really worked.

The fence and its ancillary devices came in for harsh criticisms. Whispers in the Pentagon spoke of "Bonesteel's Folly." Correspondent Wesley Pruden, Jr., remarked that "many Texas ranches have fences against frisky steers that are almost as effective." The notion of merely fencing off the ROK seemed simplistic, and the continual misadventures with the sensors only made the attempt seem more futile. Sneering mounted as the fence began to show triangular cuts six to ten inches above the ground. UNC intelligence officers estimated that it took about thirty to forty seconds for the North Koreans to cut through.[39]

Troops patrolling the rugged terrain along the DMZ

These critiques missed the mark. Bonesteel had no special love for new technology—only for new ideas. By accepting the Combat Developments Command funding and designation as a test bed, Bonesteel had to tolerate the bad with the good. At the same time, the parade of scientists pumped badly needed money and equipment into the UNC's bargain-basement war effort.

In preference to a space-age cordon, the general promoted pragmatic answers. He particularly enjoyed an idea developed in the ROK 21st Infantry Division. The enterprising Korean commander planted a hybrid strain of very light-colored buckwheat all along the fence. "You could spot something in that white area at about three times the distance you could where you didn't have the white background," observed Bonesteel. It worked quite well with the night scopes too. Plus, the ROKs harvested and ate the wheat in the autumn. Bonesteel made it a point to show the buckwheat to visiting scientists. "I was not looking for a technological solution," summarized the general.[40]

Bonesteel never expected the fence to block enemy infiltration. "It was never intended to be a barrier but was designed to hamper easy movement and provided clear observation on either side of it.... It was hard to get through one way or the other without leaving traces," said Bonesteel. These traces served to alert the other new markers on the board—the mobile quick-reaction forces (QRFs).[41]

All echelons, both U.S. and ROK, kept QRFs. They varied in size but often consisted of a reinforced squad in each forward company, a platoon at battalion level, a company at brigade, and a battalion/squadrons per division. Usually built around mechanized infantry, tanks, armored cavalry, or even the few available helicopters, these units waited—locked and loaded—to neutralize KPA intruders. The U.S. 2d Infantry Division supplemented its QRF with a five-platoon Counter Agent Company drawn from the division's KATUSAs.[42] The QRFs went to many false alarms, but they also tracked down and eliminated quite a few infiltrators.

No one part of the DMZ defenses could stem infiltration, but the sum of the four layers produced a synergistic effect that surely made KPA efforts much more daunting. The KPA had found it challenging but quite possible to slip through the old network of DMZ patrols and posts. Reinforced patrols and guard posts made that passage less sure, and the barrier fence and associated quick-reaction forces threatened dangers going in or out. All of this had been done at little monetary cost and virtually no change in the UNC's readiness for midintensity war.

Good as the system might be, the crucial barrier fence that tied it together still spanned only two divisional fronts in 1967—pending more funding. Bonesteel could not guarantee added resources sufficient to finish the fence. He could and did take actions to make all of his DMZ forces more effective, with or without the new barrier.

In response to the strong recommendations of his Special Working Group, General Bonesteel loosened the rules of engagement in early 1967. "The north Koreans were using our half of the DMZ as a kind of sanctuary," noted the general. "They'd go in and camp there for three or four nights and scout out our guard posts and the little ROK posts at the southern end of the DMZ, then they would raid them. So, we changed the rules a bit."

The UN commander in chief gave the commanding generals of I Corps (Group) and ROK First Army the authority to employ artillery and mortar fires against known enemy elements in or south of the DMZ. He also permitted these subordinates to use artillery and mortars against KPA units shooting from hostile territory. In mid-April, ROK units made use of these modifications when they fired howitzer rounds across the DMZ in response to a large KPA probe. This was the first UN use of artillery since the armistice.[43]

Bonesteel justified his changes in terms of his "overriding responsibility for taking care of the troops." When he sent a copy of his message back to Washington, he remembered: "I didn't ask for approval, but I gave them the opportunity to disapprove."[44] The Joint Chiefs and Secretary Robert S. McNamara let the new rules stand as issued.

American soldiers have always enjoyed the right of self-defense, especially on the troubled DMZ. Bonesteel's explicit new rules of engagement made it clear that U.S. troops need not wait to get shot at. Any infiltrator trying to cross the DMZ became fair game. The news made an immediate impression on the fighting front. Asked by a reporter if his men could fire on hostiles, a brigade staff officer retorted: "Yes, sir, we can and we do." Another officer explained that "we do not fire across the MDL unless fired upon. However, when North Korean troops cross the MDL, we attempt to capture or kill them."[45]

If taken in isolation, these new rules might have led to the same massive use of firepower that often pummeled snipers and infiltrators in Vietnam. This did not happen in Korea. The ROKs used significant artillery and mortar fires along the DMZ only three times during the Second Korean Conflict; they used big guns sparingly in their later counterguerrilla sweeps farther to the south. The U.S. units never employed their mighty supporting fires.[46] A number of South Korean civilians lived within artillery range of the DMZ and in the vicinity of counterinsurgent operations. Certainly, many would have suffered had things been done differently.

Why did the allies forfeit their most responsive, devastating form of combat power? Partially, this reflected the nature of combat in this conflict. Possibly for fear of retaliation from the massed, capable UN artillery, North Korean gunners on the DMZ seldom fired their own tubes unless covering the withdrawal of an agent team in contact. Sea intruders could not move rapidly inland if forced to lug bulky cannons or even mortars ashore, and KPN watercraft did not loiter to deliver fire support at clandestine drop sites. Armistice provisions also figured in, with neither side anxious to commit massive violations and provoke a midintensity war.

General Bonesteel's repeated emphasis upon stopping the northerners with manpower, not firepower, probably resulted in the UN resorting to less cannon gunnery along the DMZ and in the ROK interior. Detecting and slowing KPA agents could cause these lightly armed teams to be pinpointed and exposed to the direct fires of allied small units, which were more than able to finish off the hostiles. Even the threat of running into such responses confounded KPA planners. By making infiltration harder and by not killing North Koreans, the UN regulated its response to aggression. When it got too hard to stay covert, Bonesteel thought that Kim Il-sung would have to turn off his shadow war or risk accelerating it into conventional combat.

Artillery fires might contribute a little to the neutralization stage of anti-infiltration tactics, but in general, barraging a squad or platoon amounted to overkill, with potentially crippling side effects. The UN commander in chief's reticence to use artillery flew in the face of the American custom of "send a bullet, not a man" and might have even cost a few allied lives and wounds. But Bonesteel single-mindedly pursued his overall objective. He knew that blowing up a friendly country and its friendly populace merited little in a guerrilla struggle, even if a few more infiltrators, or a few less friendlies, died. Keeping the allegiance of the South Koreans mattered more than kill ratios. "I wasn't much for body count," remarked Bonesteel.[47] The UN's big guns remained silent.

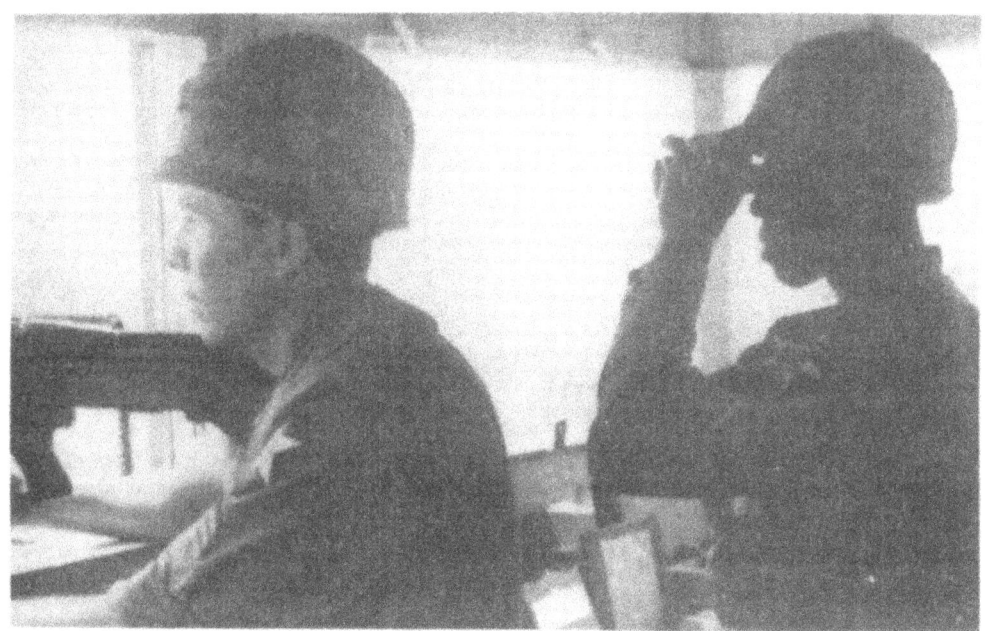

Watchful members of Company C, 3d Battalion, 23d Infantry, survey the DMZ for infiltrators

In addition to tactical innovations and liberalized rules of engagement, Bonesteel also ensured that his DMZ divisions instituted a sensible DMZ training and rotation plan (see figure 7). Here again, the general followed the recommendations of his Special Working Group. The unique aspects of the DMZ required special, intensive training, especially in light of the Americans' usual problems with personnel turbulence and inexperienced leaders. Conversely, units stuck on the DMZ too long might lose their ability to maneuver on a midintensity battlefield. Saddled with both the low-intensity and midintensity missions, the U.S. and ROK armies compromised and went with an orderly rotation. Mandatory, exhaustive pre-DMZ training, to include orientation patrols in the zone for small-unit leaders, reduced the vulnerability of newly arrived battalions on the zone. Each battalion also was exposed to only its "fair share" of DMZ danger—an important morale consideration.

As they trained for the DMZ, units mounted local patrols in the vicinity of their camps. These were not just dull practice runs; a threat to the rear, though not as bad as on the zone, really existed. North Korean terrorist bombings, minings, and snipping—exemplified by the May 1967 demolition of an American barracks—helped make all patrols important. Units in depth, like the U.S. 7th Infantry Division, grew especially adept at conducting these security measures.

In the process, both U.S. and ROK forces sharpened their battle focus throughout their forward unit areas, keeping all battalions actively involved, not just the forward units and QRFs. Consequently, terrorist strikes dropped off in 1968, even though other types of incidents peaked in that violent

---

**Training**

| Week | 0 | Battalion notified of upcoming DMZ duty. |
|---|---|---|
| Weeks | 1—7 | Squad/platoon training; weapons qualification; "Quick Kill" courses; patrolling techniques. |
| Weeks | 8—13 | Company/battalion exercises; Expert Infantryman's Badge Test; Battalion Operational Readiness Test (including 17- to 25-mile foot march). |
| Weeks | 14—16 | Barrier operations; DMZ reaction/orientation course; night firing; sniper marksmanship; division command inspection. |

**Rotation Rules**

1. Each battalion served about four months.
2. One new battalion relieved the most "senior" DMZ battalion each full-moon phase (about once a month).
3. The brigade headquarters (3d Brigade, U.S. 2d Infantry Division and "4th Brigade" [actually 2d Brigade, U.S. 7th Infantry Division] did not rotate.
4. The U.S. 2d Infantry Division Quick-Reaction Force was often located in the area of operations of the DMZ brigades and usually operated under the operational control of a forward brigade.

Sources: United States Army, 2d Infantry Division, 3d Brigade, "Annual Historical Supplement 1968"; United States Army, 2d Infantry Division, 2d Brigade, "Annual Historical Supplement 1969"; and Colonel William R. Guthrie, United States Army, "Korea: The Other DMZ," *Infantry* 60 (March-April 1970):18.

---

Figure 7. U.S. manuever battalion DMZ training and rotation plan (initiated October 1967)

year. The allies fully exploited training patrols to promote rear-area security and thus quelled the terrorist challenge while increasing proficiency for the primary DMZ task.

In the U.S. sector, these changes went into effect during the autumn. One more battalion, drawn from the U.S. 7th Infantry Division, joined the 3d Brigade, U.S. 2d Infantry Division, along the zone. This beefed up U.S. forces to four frontline battalions and one QRF.[48] ROK units took similar measures. Even allowing for this modest increase of strength in and along the DMZ, the vast majority of U.S. Eighth Army's subordinate I Corps (Group) and ROK First Army remained off the zone, ready to deal with a conventional ground invasion.

## Anti-Infiltration: The Sea Approaches

Unlike the effort to contain infiltration along the DMZ, the fight against sea intruders portended nothing but headaches. The Republic of Korea's coruscated coasts stretched almost twenty-eight times the length of the DMZ—an incredible frontier to try to protect. Without any U.S. Navy or Coast Guard ships at his disposal, and with his U.S. Air Force squadrons busy watching for a North Korean air strike, General Bonesteel had to rely almost wholly on the ROKs to do the mission.

This sort of sea operation was not merely a variation on a conventional mission. It bore little resemblance to normal U.S. Navy tasks. In America, such duties devolve upon the Coast Guard and local police forces. U.S. sailors had their hands full trying to generate a coastal interdiction capability off Vietnamese shores. Few human or material resources could be spared for Korea.[49] Bonesteel's tiny U.S. Navy component could offer little in the way of relevant advice or equipment.

Bonesteel was no sailor, but he recognized the broad outlines of the problem. With the help of U.S. and ROK seamen, airmen, and soldiers, he went to work. Halting infiltration by water required a sea barrier, a land-based detection system to identify infiltrators, some means of local defense to fix the enemy, and on-call QRFs to finish the job.[50] Some parts of these systems existed, although not always in useful form.

The sea barrier sought to sort enemy craft from among the hundreds of South Korean fishing vessels that plied the ROK coasts. An ideal system would feature long-duration radar-equipped patrol planes (like the U.S. Navy's P-3 Orion) ranging out to 100 kilometers. Ground-based coastal radar, scanning out to twenty kilometers, backed up these aircraft. The planes and radars would handle initial detection and pass suspicious surface contacts on to patrol boats working twenty to sixty kilometers out. Heliborne boarding parties and fighter-bombers on strip alert waited, ready to join the fray if the patrol boats needed help. Such an integrated structure depended upon a lot of communications and reliable radars.[51]

In 1967, South Korea's sea barrier consisted mainly of the small ROK Navy. This force totaled a paltry seventy-two vessels—only about half in any way suited for coastal duties. The ROK Air Force also stood ready to dispatch a few flights of jet fighter-bombers when called. Neither service had long-duration patrol planes, advanced radars, or adequate communications. Only a few coastal radar sites existed, mostly near ROK or U.S. Navy facilities.[52]

The sea barrier provided a nuisance to infiltrators, but distinguishing friend from foe confounded the ROKs even in those cases where they thought they had targets. Pitched engagements with intruders rarely occurred. The only solid success of 1967 came in April, when navy (ROKN) patrol boats and air force (ROKAF) fighters cooperated to sink a North Korean espionage vessel.[53] In the main, though, the ROK sea barrier was an ambitious enterprise that could not directly suppress infiltration.

Land-based detection relied mainly on about 200,000 unarmed coast watchers who reported to the National Police. These local people, occasionally supplemented by ROK Army reservists, patrolled the beachfronts. They rarely detected any landings in progress but often found traces of landings that activated reaction forces and led to kills and captures. In June, coast watchers near Samchok found one of the KPN's specially designed agent boats stranded on the shore. Clues from this boat led to a massive search, unearthed a talkative prisoner, and unmasked other operatives.[54]

The unarmed coast watchers could detect, but they could hardly hope to engage, armed special forces teams. In 1967, no armed local units were on hand to delay intruders until regulars arrived. Provincial police lacked the firepower, mobility, training, and numbers to do the job.[55] Many trails grew cold while diligent watchmen waited for help to arrive.

A village militia, like that in the DPRK, could have provided this missing piece to the anti-infiltration puzzle. But with demonstrations and rioting in Seoul during the May—June 1967 elections and clear indications of a northern guerrilla effort under way, President Park showed an understandable reluctance to issue arms to the general populace. Instead, the ROKs relied on military quick-reaction forces. By late 1967, these included ROK Army regulars, reservists, and men of the hundred-odd new Combat Police companies organized from the National Police ranks.[56]

With few helicopters and few communications links (either radio or telephone) to the coast watchers or each other, these strong forces hardly ever arrived in time to catch KPA infiltration teams before they dispersed. The ROKs fragmented command between the disparate agencies involved, which discouraged speedy reactions. Kills and captures resulted—but only after prodigious expenditures of time and resources and often only with the loan of the few available American Huey helicopters.[57]

Sea infiltration could not be stopped, but the interlopers could be tracked and eliminated—if the ROK properly coordinated its activities. The humble coast watchers exemplified the sort of solution that might make up for missing radars and absent patrol planes. But in 1967, the Korean government was not yet ready to go that route.

## *Counterinsurgency: The Interior*

The Samchok agent boat gave the first hard evidence that the northerners had begun earnest preparations for the third and decisive phase of Kim Il-sung's unconventional campaign. "They [Kim's agents] were targeted against a specific region or province of the south. They were developing, in effect, an infrastructure, the gauleiters, the pseudo-government officials," concluded Bonesteel.[58]

The South Koreans immediately recognized the hazard. Alarmed, they turned to the Americans. Bonesteel remembered: "They pretty much wanted CINCUNC to be responsible for anti-agent activities all over the country." The general flatly rejected this. "I reminded them," he said, "they were a sovereign country, and I, as the UN commander, was only responsible for the DMZ and the sea approaches. However, internal security was their responsibility." With that statement, Bonesteel reaffirmed the U.S. policy in effect since 1950.[59]

As tempting as full authority might have appeared, General Bonesteel knew it was an illusion. Most likely, once they saw the true magnitude of the measures necessary, the ROKs would not cede to an American the degree of domestic political power essential to meet an incipient insurgency. Bonesteel could end up with responsibility without authority, and the ROK government, thinking that the UNC was doing the job, might well become dangerously vulnerable to North Korea's unconventional campaign.

But what if the ROKs awarded Bonesteel unprecedented prerogatives? That might well provide an even better opening for the DPRK. Kim Il-sung, who regularly charged Bonesteel with such dictatorial powers anyway, would point to the situation as proof that Park's administration really was composed of nothing but puppets. Thus, Kim could declare himself the only true Korean nationalist, an assertion hard for Park to refute with an American general running much of his country. That might have been enough to sway sympathies in the ROK villages.

So Bonesteel stuck to material assistance and advice. He loaned his allies his precious helicopters and U.S. communications equipment. He even parceled out a few valuable A-Teams, coaxed during the summer from the 1st Special Forces on Okinawa; the Green Berets worked in the Taebaek and southern Chiri Mountain regions.[60] But the American general adamantly refused to run this internal war for the South Koreans.

ROK counterinsurgency operations, while not lacking in enthusiasm or scale, granted the initiative to the Communists. Throwing unit after unit of regulars and police at possible contacts made sense as long as the contacts remained few in number and uncoordinated with DPRK conventional threats. Both of those variables looked certain to change for the worse as

Kim Il-sung's forces shifted into the guerrilla uprising phase of their campaign plan. Confused command structures, lack of dedicated counterinsurgency units, and a purely reactive mind-set all conspired to render the vigorous ROK operations inefficient and, too often, ineffective. During his frequent meetings with President Park, Ministry of Defense officials, intelligence directors, and ROK armed forces chiefs, Bonesteel urged them to unify command of the counterguerrilla effort. The ROKs politely listened but continued in their own way. "They made some mistakes," admitted Bonesteel.

As it was, ROK Army commanders and National Police officials alternately took charge of ad hoc task forces, depending upon the initial estimate of the threat and who happened to be nearby. Army counterintelligence and the Korean CIA ran independent missions, only occasionally consulting with the army or police. While not the best way to do business against guerrillas, this diffused arrangement nicely balanced the key power brokers in Park's administration, allowing each a piece of the action.[61]

For the same reason, the ROKs chose not to establish any special counterinsurgency units. Which agency would get the new forces, and how would they affect that agency's influence in state affairs? These were important considerations. Besides, the current delicate balance seemed to be getting the job done. To date, the army-police lash-up had worked, just as it had from 1950—53.[62]

Finally, the ROK government responded to North Korean insurgent threats as they arose. No concerted effort mobilized the South Korean people against the guerrilla organizers. Park and his lieutenants failed to link their military and police operations with an alternative mass movement to counter Kim Il-sung's *Juche* ideology (a Korean nationalist interpretation of Marx, Lenin, and Mao).

Park and his men expected their people to report irregularities. Still, Park chose not to trust his citizens to defend themselves. Unarmed and mostly uninformed, the people posed no threat to Park—but neither did they threaten outside agitators. Having created a coup and seen plenty of public unrest, Park played it safe. In doing so, however, he missed an early opportunity to harness the energies of what turned out to be a very loyal population.[63] He would correct this oversight under dire pressure early in 1968.

Yet the lessons learned in counterinsurgent warfare during 1967 did not go unrecorded or unanalyzed—far from it. Bonesteel and Park coordinated to produce two important documents near the end of 1967. Together, the UNC Counterinfiltration-Guerrilla Concept Requirements Plan and the ROK Presidential Instruction #18 charted the future course of combined operations against DPRK unconventional pressures.

The UNC plan codified all of the successful improvisations of the year. It addressed the DMZ, the coasts, and the interior. The core of the plan lay in its forecasts of necessary items: helicopters, radios, xenon searchlights, night-vision devices, and the vital chain-link fencing. If someone asked, Bonesteel had his shopping list ready. In 1967, nobody was asking.

The ROK presidential instruction tied into the UNC plan. It showed that all of Bonesteel's arguments and suggestions had not fallen on deaf ears. When implemented in full, his instruction would remedy the command controversies and lack of dedicated counterinsurgency formations. Park directed the establishment of a national coordinating council to reduce command friction. Under this concept, even the previously unfettered intelligence people came to heel. The president spelled out clear chains of command for all classes of incidents ranging from individual agent sightings to province-level unrest. The ROK president also ordered the creation of eight (later ten) new ROK Army counterinfiltration battalions, as well as further expansion of the new Combat Police. He stopped short of authorizing a popular militia, however.

In the words of Bonesteel's aide, Lieutenant Colonel Walter B. Clark, "Presidential Instruction #18 was a total systems approach to the infiltration problem." This all required several months to fall completely into place, but important decisions had been made.

So the Americans needed money, and the South Koreans needed time. Despite painful casualties suffered in the learning process, the Republic of Korea remained intact and strong. Bonesteel thought they were on the right course. He would find out soon enough, as the Second Korean Conflict moved to its climax in the cold snows of a grim January.

# *A Continuous Nightmare* 3

> Communist north Korea has made 1968 the bloodiest year in Korea since 1953.
>
> —Gilbert H. Woodward
> Major General, U.S. Army,
> representative at Panmunjom, 1968

Allied losses in 1967 increased dramatically in comparison to previous years. In accord with Kim Il-sung's new intent, Americans suffered some especially sharp reverses both on patrols and in their rear areas, with sixteen killed and more than fifty wounded. ROK casualties also climbed to over 100 killed and more than 200 wounded. About seventy-five South Koreans died or fell injured in fighting around their villages.[1]

Still, while a matter of great concern to both the Americans and the ROKs, these losses had not caused either country's government to question the validity of their alliance. In fact, General Bonesteel and President Park seemed to be working more closely together than ever. Their military forces showed signs of developing useful anti-infiltration and counterguerrilla capabilities. At the same time, the ROK populace remained, at best, apathetic toward the North Korean interlopers and far more often were exceedingly hostile.

What was going wrong? Due to lack of numbers, Kim Il-sung's covert forces simply could not mount an unconventional offensive on the scale necessary to shake the United Nations Command. Nor had the KPA proved adept at striking at sensitive targets certain to generate U.S.-ROK discord. Most of the attacks simply struck average American and ROK soldiers. Although more energetic and bloody, the escapades to date still lacked organization and focus, the same problems that plagued the 1962—66 political agitation campaign. The KPA generals had delivered a great many disjointed operations but had made precious little progress.

Indeed, the KPA-led campaign was creating an even worse situation than the previous political effort. North Korean special operators had neither driven off the Yankees nor subverted the ROK farmers. Rather, the KPA men had done just enough to galvanize the Americans and South Koreans into taking the kinds of strong measures that would, if completed, spell the end of any chance for decisive DPRK unconventional operations. Moreover, Kim's goal of a South Korean uprising seemed to be slipping further away with each new meter of barrier fence built and each coast-watcher cell organized.

But Kim Il-sung was not yet ready to give up on his three-phase campaign. After all, many of the North Korean's more potent stratagems still waited on the drawing board, approved but unfunded, recognized but not yet implemented. If the North Koreans acted promptly and chose their targets carefully, they could still damage the U.S.-ROK alliance and create the preconditions for victory in the south.

The DPRK could turn to new forces to carry out this renewed effort against the south. Chief among these were the plainly titled 124th and 283d Army Units, which were in fact unique outfits raised and schooled specifically to carry out Kim Il-sung's unconventional campaign. Each unit numbered about a thousand men, all officers, all handpicked. They coalesced around a chain of command chosen from the most experienced veterans of the foot reconnaissance brigades.

The two units each fielded nine subunits, with every subunit targeted on one of the nine major ROK provinces. Members of the units trained intensively to gain familiarity with their assigned areas. The officers readied themselves for direct-action roles and for recruitment and organization of South Korean guerrillas. Alongside their provincially focused elements, both formations retained separate teams for special missions of strategic significance to the DPRK leadership.[2]

One such mission arose on 5 January 1968, well past the date when the DMZ settled into its usual winter torpor. A 31-man detachment from the 124th Army Unit went into isolation in Sariwon, where they began to rehearse a building seizure and assassination sequence. For eight days, the team studied sanitized maps of a hypothetical objective and ran through numerous practice exercises concerning various key events. They had been on many such exercises since reporting to the 124th back in March of 1967. This one, however, was no war game. That became obvious on 13 January, when the team staged forward into the 6th Infantry Division's rear area, only a few kilometers north of the DMZ. KPA Reconnaissance Bureau chief, Lieutenant General Kim Chong-tae, met the men. "Your mission," he said, "is to go to Seoul and cut off the head of Park Chung Hee."[3]

## The Blue House Raid

The officers on the detachment knew that their mission might well decide the outcome of the Second Korean Conflict. North Korean Lieutenant Kim Shin Jo, a participant captured during the mission, explained that killing the ROK president "would create political problems within the South Korean government and would agitate the South Korean people to fight with arms against their government and the American imperialists."[4] With one stroke, the spearhead group of the 124th Army Unit might push the Republic of Korea into chaos and open the way for reunification from the north.

Late on the evening of 17 January, the team changed into ROK Army uniforms, donned dark coveralls, and penetrated the U.S. 2d Infantry Division sector. They cut several holes through the famous chain-link fence and slipped the entire group through, all within thirty meters of a manned U.S. position. They moved carefully for two days and nights through the American division's sector. The North Koreans even camped the second night on a forested hillside within a few kilometers of Camp Howze, the U.S. divisional headquarters.

The infiltration went smoothly until the afternoon of 19 January, when the team unexpectedly encountered four South Korean woodcutters. Seizing on an opportunity to impart a bit of indoctrination to these representatives of the ROK's "oppressed masses," the special operators harangued the terrified woodcutters about the coming insurrection and the glories of North Korean communism. At the same time, they apparently gave some inference as to the nature of their impending raid.

After a few hours, the KPA officers released the woodsmen unharmed with a stern warning not to go to the police. The special forces leaders calculated that their assassination mission was within hours of completion and that the civilians would probably not go to the police immediately, nor would the authorities believe such a wild tale.

This proved to be a fatal mistake on their part. The South Koreans went to the police that very night. The local police chief believed them and notified his chain of command, which reacted promptly in accord with Presidential Instruction #18. By morning, the ROK's new counterguerrilla structure commenced operations.[5] Unfortunately, the ROK leadership did not know the exact mission of the 124th Army Unit, so the police and the military tried to guard all important sites and at the same time search the approaches to Seoul. Even with massive resources employed, however, the ROKs could not cover everything.

The stealthy raiders entered the city in two- and three-man cells on 20 January. They quickly became aware of the frenzied atmosphere in the capital. Eavesdropping on busy police and ROK Army radio nets, the KPA team's leaders plotted the identities and movements of their foes. Obviously, the original plan had to be abandoned. The 124th Army Unit would have to improvise. The North Koreans were well trained, and their commander saw a possible way to make use of the heightened alert. Maybe they could still complete their mission.

Upon rendezvous that night, the men removed their coveralls. This revealed their ROK Army uniforms, complete with the correct unit insignia of the local ROK 26th Infantry Division. The team then formed up and prepared to march the last mile to the Blue House, the ROK presidential residence, posing as ROK Army soldiers returning from a counterguerrilla patrol.

A tracker dog from the U.S. 2d Infantry Division trains for its anti-intruder role on the DMZ

The platoon marched smartly toward the Blue House, passing several National Police and ROK Army units en route. A scant 800 meters from the Blue House, a police contingent finally halted the platoon and began to ask questions that exceeded anything the raiders had rehearsed. The nervous North Koreans fumbled their replies. One suspicious policeman drew his pistol; a commando shot him. A melee then ensued in which two 124th men died.[6] The rest of the North Koreans scattered and began racing for the DMZ.

ROK soldiers, police, and American troops cooperated in the massive manhunt that followed over the next few days. Several sharp encounters flared as the desperate North Koreans clawed their way toward home. Three more operatives were pursued and killed in the Seoul area. Subsequently, aroused I Corps (Group) units—to include both U.S. divisions—participated in successful sweeps that killed twenty-three and captured one of the North Koreans. Only two of the thirty-one northerners could not be accounted for—and they were presumed dead.

The liquidation of the Blue House assault team, however, came at a horrendous price. Three Americans died and three fell wounded in attempts to block the escaping infiltrators. ROK casualties totaled sixty-eight killed and sixty-six wounded—mainly army and police but also about two dozen hapless civilians.[7] This cost hardly served as a ringing endorsement for all the security improvements developed and instituted throughout 1967.

Much had gone very wrong. The 124th cut right through the heart of the most developed segment of the DMZ barrier system. The embarrassing inattentiveness of the U.S. 2d Infantry Division said little for American military performance and strained U.S.-ROK relations. Indeed, the key event in the whole process revolved around a chance meeting with unarmed timbermen—random players not really part of the United Nations Command's anti-infiltration scheme. Fortunately for President Park, the loyal civilians notified the police, and the local authorities acted with alacrity. Had the KPA killed the woodcutters, the infiltrators might well have killed Park too. Even in the teeth of an alerted Seoul, the enemy nevertheless closed to within 800 meters of Park's residence, stopped more by luck and individual initiative than by a grand design.

Much had also gone right. The citizenry responded, the police foiled the raid, and a hasty but thorough amalgam of quick-reaction forces relentlessly pursued the North Koreans. The 124th Army Unit had gotten in, but they could not get back out—a tribute to the DMZ enhancements. In terms of anti-infiltration methodology, the delay and neutralization efforts had gone pretty well. Detection, however, still relied too much on the thin crust of regular forces along the DMZ. Most of the casualties occurred during attempts to track down the intruders. The allies were still finding too many of their prey only while being ambushed.

Nobody had much of a chance to reflect on lessons learned. U.S. and ROK soldiers were still tracking down the remnants of the Blue House raiding detachment when, as Bonesteel recalled, "the damned *Pueblo* occurred two days later and that really put the fat in the fire."[8]

## The "Damned Pueblo"

Neither General Bonesteel nor the South Koreans knew anything about the USS *Pueblo* (AGER-2), an American electronic surveillance ship operating off the east coast of the DPRK in January 1968. The United Nations Command forces, like most of the world, first heard of the small vessel when it surrendered to KPN patrol boats and KPAF MiGs on 23 January 1968. One American died during the boarding; eighty-two entered North Korean captivity. The ship was then anchored in Wonsan harbor.

Officially, the USS *Pueblo* did not concern Bonesteel until it was captured and thereby entered his area of operations. He had warned the intelligence agencies and the Seventh Fleet about previous activities near Wonsan, but nobody had paid much attention to him.[9] Now, Bonesteel was compelled to worry about it. After the capture, any UNC response to the Blue House raid had to take into account eighty-two unlucky American sailors.

The best chance to help the defenseless *Pueblo* passed during the afternoon of 23 January, as Seventh Fleet, Fifth Air Force, and U.S. Forces, Korea, attempted to sort out what was happening. The small ship, responding to various intelligence agencies and operating on the fringes of the Seventh Fleet-U.S. Forces, Korea, areas, really did not "belong" to anyone. Neither the U.S. Air Force nor the U.S. Navy had set aside any air cover for the ship, and their understrength local units could not scramble enough of the right type of planes in time to drive off the *Pueblo*'s tormentors.

In theory, Bonesteel's 314th Air Division and the ROKs had the power to intervene. But they were fully involved in the post-Blue House sweeps, vigilant to thwart any follow-up North Korean attacks, and had no prior knowledge of the *Pueblo* mission. Indeed, Bonesteel found out about the capture "just as it was happening."

The USS *Pueblo*

Admiral Ulysses S. G. Sharp, Commander in Chief, U.S. Pacific Command

When he turned to his U.S. Air Force commander, he found that the only seven aircraft ready and capable of reaching Wonsan carried fittings strictly suited for nuclear bombs. If the ground crews changed them over or readied other planes, they would be too late to prevent the ship from reaching Wonsan. On its part, the ROK Air Force could range all the way to Wonsan only with the most lightly armed fighters—and then only by violating DPRK airspace, a risky proposition in light of recent events.[10]

Nightfall sealed the fate of the *Pueblo* and her unhappy crew. American leaders fumed, raged, and wondered what to do. Some civilians in the White House and State and Defense Departments talked about blockading Wonsan, telling the ROKs to grab a Soviet spy ship, or even initiating "warning" air raids that would fly right up to the Wonsan area with all radars operating before angling off. But what about the ship's crewmen? That was always the rub.

Involved military men advocated the sternest possible response, fearful of the bad precedent being set and wary of the effects on the already edgy ROKs. Admiral Ulysses S. Grant Sharp, the Commander in Chief, U.S. Pacific Command, proposed sailing the destroyer USS *Higbee* (DD-806) straight into Wonsan harbor, covered by the aircraft of the carrier USS *Enterprise* (CVAN-65).[11] The *Higbee* would demand release of the *Pueblo* and its crew, promising air strikes on Wonsan if unheeded.

Bonesteel's idea was even harsher. Already fully enmeshed in the aftermath of the Blue House raid, the general reacted with uncharacteristic

Military operations during the Tet Offensive in Vietnam

emotion at this latest North Korean affront: "It was a most inexcusable and infuriating thing," he said. His patience exhausted, Bonesteel argued for a blunt nuclear ultimatum against Kim Il-sung: release the *Pueblo* or else.[12]

It was the strongest measure ever suggested by Bonesteel and quite possibly the strongest course of action ever recommended by any U.S. theater commander during the nuclear age. If nothing else, it offers an indication of how much pressure rode on Bonesteel's shoulders in January of 1968. The insertion of eighty-two American hostages into an already highly charged and dangerous DPRK-UNC confrontation had, at least for a few hours, brought the normally intellectual Bonesteel to the brink of irrationality.

Nothing came of Bonesteel's suggestions nor that of the others for that matter. On 30—31 January 1968, the Vietnamese Communists launched their massive Tet Offensive, and the Korean crisis had to take a backseat to a full-scale war.

## *The Moment of Crisis*

The last week or so of January 1968 offered enough problems for a dozen American presidents—let alone an already haggard Lyndon Johnson. On 20 January, U.S. Marines repulsed a heavy attack on the hills surrounding their vulnerable Khe Sanh combat base; a steady artillery barrage began the next day. On 21 January, reports of the Blue House raid reached Washington. On 22 January, a B-52 bomber crashed off Greenland, spilling four nuclear weapons into the icy waters. On 23 January, the *Pueblo* was lost. On 29 January, Johnson had to announce a large tax increase to finance the Vietnam War. On 30—31 January, the great Tet Offensive swept across South Vietnam, simultaneously rocking the major cities and even briefly threatening the U.S. Embassy compound. Johnson wrote later: "I sometimes felt that I was living in a continuous nightmare."[13]

For Johnson, it would get worse, especially in Vietnam. By this time, the president considered almost every issue in relation to the war in Southeast Asia. He focused on the *Pueblo* and Tet Offensive—not the Blue House raid. Johnson assumed the North Korean seizure of the *Pueblo* to be closely coordinated with the Tet attack and evidence of a Communist master plot: "They were trying to divert U.S. military resources from Vietnam," explained Johnson. He guessed that Kim Il-sung was "trying to pressure the South Koreans into recalling their two divisions from that area (Vietnam)." If his memoirs are any indicator, Johnson really believed that strange, improbable contention.[14]

At this point, the American president still hoped for a favorable outcome in Vietnam and seemed determined not to widen the hostilities in Korea—regardless of the *Pueblo*. Rather than threaten reprisal, Johnson decided to deal with the devil to get his men back. He ordered Bonesteel to approach the DPRK through the Military Armistice Commission at Panmunjom, the only channel of contact between America and North Korea. The ROKs, who were represented by the United Nations Command in the commission meetings at Panmunjom, were not consulted.[15]

President Park and his advisers also narrowed their focus. For them, Tet was a sideshow. The raid on the Blue House and the taking of the USS *Pueblo* demonstrated the magnitude of the North Korean threat—a menace that called for the strongest possible riposte from *both* allies. Newspaper editorials and government officials remarked that perhaps the ROK must bring its troops home from Vietnam to meet the new Communist peril. This chorus of opinion grew more strident once rumors of direct U.S.-DPRK negotiations reached Seoul. Angry ROK Defense Minister Kim Song-un charged Bonesteel with conscious duplicity in the affair. On 6 February, the ROKs lodged an official protest against their U.S. ally, accusing the Americans of a "policy of appeasement." An enraged President Park refused to negotiate seriously with General Bonesteel or Ambassador William J. Porter. The ROK leader demanded immediate dispatch of a new emissary empowered to speak for President Johnson.[16]

Many opinion leaders in the south urged Park to "go north"—with or without the Americans. ROK generals bragged openly of their inclinations to interpret rules of engagement to permit "hot pursuit all the way to the Yalu River." Concerned by this bellicose talk, Ambassador Porter cabled a warning that "Park might take some unpredictable action, such as an attack on north Korea." An embassy official later told reporter Emerson Chapin that the South Koreans hovered "very close" to war.[17] Kim Il-sung's raiders had failed, but the attempt alone, combined with other circumstances, was creating the kind of U.S.-ROK split long desired by the DPRK.

In the middle of all of this controversy sat Bonesteel, the very man who had just recommended nuclear threats to regain control of the USS *Pueblo*. Where would he stand in relation to his country's president—who wanted to do whatever he could to avoid midintensity war in Korea—and his ally's president—who appeared to be itching to start that same war?

The emotional Bonesteel had already lashed out, but now with the moment of crisis at hand, the relentlessly logical Bonesteel took over. He made a quick but thorough study of Tet, the Blue House raid, and the *Pueblo* seizure, searching for connections. He found none. Only the assassination attempt appeared to have been preplanned in Pyongyang. Tet was coincidental but helpful, the *Pueblo* a gift that the DPRK had gladly snatched and exploited.

It looked like the North Koreans had been aware of Tet but launched the Blue House raid in conformity with their own schedule. If Tet served to distract America and fix South Korean forces in distant Vietnam, all the better. The Blue House attack was clearly designed to force issues on the peninsula, not tie in with some Vietnamese operation. Lyndon Johnson's conviction that Kim Il-sung acted to spur an ROK withdrawal from Southeast Asia makes little sense. More ROK infantry on the Korean peninsula surely was the last thing Kim wanted.

As for the *Pueblo*, it certainly benefited the North Koreans to hold U.S. prisoners. Even so, the attack on the U.S. ship looked opportunistic, perhaps even initiated by an overly aggressive local commander. The attack followed a long series of similar DPRK acts against various American and South Korean vessels and aircraft. This pattern, stretching back to 1953, predated the Second Korean Conflict.[18] It was unlikely that Kim Il-sung planned the seizure, but once he had the ship, he certainly knew how to use it and its crew to create contention between the Americans and their ROK allies.

Based upon this analysis of the situation, Bonesteel fell back on his unchanged, two-fold mission: to defend the ROK, while avoiding a second major Asian war. Bonesteel resolved that the American determination to avoid a major war had to be reflected in a restated and strengthened commitment to deterring the bigger war, while winning the low-intensity conflict in progress on the Korean peninsula. The South Korean ardor for vengeance had to be transformed into actions that precluded a rerun of the Blue House raid.[19] If General Bonesteel handled it correctly, this crisis could become an opportunity.

## The Conventional Response: A Show of Force

In reacting to the Korean crisis, President Johnson and his key subordinates borrowed from Theodore Roosevelt. America spoke softly to the South Koreans, while carrying a much bigger stick than usual in the waters and air near the DPRK. This stick provided leverage over both Koreas. Concerned about a North Korean drive to take advantage of the U.S.-ROK indecision and discord, President Johnson ordered a massive contingency deployment of American sea and air power in the Korean theater (see figure 8). Ground reinforcements were not sent. "We assumed that the South Korean Army could look after itself," wrote the president. "We moved as much military power into South Korea as we could without diverting units from Southeast Asia," Johnson recalled. This increase of forces continued even as Tet broke out in Vietnam.[20]

With the Southeast Asian war already stretching the U.S. active components to their limits, the president called up 14,787 U.S. Air Force and U.S. Navy reservists to replace those forces deployed to Korea. Korea, not Tet, forced Johnson to announce a formal, partial mobilization, the first since the 1962 Cuban missile crisis. While most of the reservists remained in the United States, about 3,000 airmen eventually made it to Korea.[21]

The air power arrived under the operation code-named Combat Fox. Spurred by Lieutenant General Seth J. McKee of Fifth Air Force, several air units arrived in Korea before 1 February 1968. Along with forces from Okinawa, these included the three, potent F-4D Phantom II squadrons of Colonel Charles E. ("Chuck") Yeager's 4th Tactical Fighter Wing. Yeager's "suitcase air force" flew in from North Carolina within seventy-two hours of notification, a truly remarkable performance. Altogether, almost 200 combat aircraft deployed.[22]

At sea, the Seventh Fleet marshaled some thirty-five major surface combatants. Six aircraft carriers led the procession of naval might that comprised Operation Formation Star. Navy air furnished another 400 or so frontline combat jets.[23]

The buildup looked impressive, but appearances could be deceiving. Bonesteel had asked for this show of strength, but he did not really command it. Narrowly defined command relationships strictly limited these contingency forces to a deterrent role. Thanks to his personal influence,

### Operation Formation Star

Task Group 77.5
    USS *Enterprise* (CVAN-65) with air wing
    USS *Truxtun* (DLGN-35)
    USS *Halsey* (DLG-23)
    USS *O'Bannon* (DD-450)
    USS *Collett* (DD-730)
    USS *Higbee* (DD-806)
    USS *Ozbourn* (DD-846)

Reinforcing Elements, Seventh Fleet
    USS *Ticonderoga* (CVA-14)
    USS *Coral Sea* (CVA-43)
    USS *Ranger* (CVA-61)
    USS *Yorktown* (CVS-10)
    USS *Kearsarge* (CVS-33)
    USS *Canberra* (CA-70)
    USS *Chicago* (CG-11)
    USS *Providence* (CLG-6)
    (Thirteen other destroyer types)

### Operation Combat Fox

Fifth Air Force Advance Echelon to Osan AB (from Fuchu AS, Japan)
4th Tactical Fighter Wing to Kunsan AB (72 F-4Ds from Seymour Johnson AFB, North Carolina)
18th Tactical Fighter Wing (−) to Osan AB, Kwangju ROKAFB (36 F-105Ds from Kadena AB, Okinawa)
    12th Tactical Fighter Squadron (−) to Osan AB (12 F-105Ds from Kadena AB, Okinawa)
    334th Tactical Fighter Squadron to Kwangju ROKAFB (24 105-Ds from Kadena AB, Okinawa)
64th Fighter-Interceptor Squadron to Kimpo AB (24 F-102As from Naha AB, Okinawa)
82d Fighter-Interceptor Squadron to Suwon ROKAFB (24 F-102As from Naha AB, Okinawa)
318th Fighter-Interceptor Squadron to Osan AB (24 F-106As from McChord AFB, Washington)

### *Abbreviations*

| | | | |
|---|---|---|---|
| AB | air base | CVAN | nuclear-powered CVA |
| AFB | Air Force Base | CVS | antisubmarine aircraft carrier |
| AS | air station | DD | destroyer |
| CA | heavy cruiser | DLG | guided missile DD leader |
| CG | guided missile cruiser | DLGN | nuclear-powered DLG |
| CLG | guided missile light cruiser | ROKAFB | Republic of Korea AFB |
| CVA | attack aircraft carrier | | |

Figure 8. The United States' military response to the seizure of the USS *Pueblo*, January through March 1968

Bonesteel received some help from the Fifth Air Force in prosecuting the Second Korean Conflict; the Seventh Fleet did not cooperate at all.

The Fifth Air Force's Advance Echelon took charge of the U.S. Air Force's (USAF) contribution. Senior USAF officers made it clear that these air units "[were] neither assigned nor attached to the command of General Bonesteel as Commander, US Forces Korea." In the event of an overt invasion, the Fifth Air Force would come under UN authority. But until then, it responded to distant U.S. Pacific Air Forces and through them to U.S. Pacific Command.

Fortunately, Generals McKee and Bonesteel worked out practical arrangements to make use of the new air units in the ongoing low-intensity conflict. Combat Fox aircraft aided the ROKs in sea-approach coverage and provided strip-alert quick-reaction flights. Both American infantry divisions received and exercised new forward air controller teams and procedures, although no actual air strikes occurred. Squadrons and wings rotated to Korea at regular intervals, allowing some training for them from the commitment. Once the imminent danger subsided, the USAF component gradually pared back to its precrisis strength. In all, Combat Fox lasted sixteen months.[24]

The U.S. Navy went its own way, with the Seventh Fleet anxious to reduce the task groups and speed ships to Vietnamese waters. None of the warships responded to General Bonesteel in any capacity, although he would gain some air sorties in the event of a major war. For Seventh Fleet, the Korean circuit mainly constituted a waste of time. According to one participating admiral, these activities "usually involved some rather innocuous air operations for a couple of days, using one of our aircraft carriers."[25] By summer, the Seventh Fleet had moved on.

Although not fully orchestrated for maximum support of General Bonesteel's UNC, the contingency buildup worked. This tremendous show

Charles E. ("Chuck") Yeager in a Bell X-1 supersonic aircraft. Yeager led three squadrons of F-4Ds into Korea in response to the *Pueblo* seizure

of force brought in ten times the amount of aircraft normally operated by the 314th Air Division. The 600 or so USAF and U.S. Navy (USN) jets completely negated the only real conventional edge the DPRK possessed—their air arm. Any northern blitzkrieg would have to proceed under American-dominated skies. North Korea did not try anything. Even unconventional operations dwindled in the face of the U.S. air and sea armadas.

Thus, the contingency deployments did their job and guaranteed some breathing space for the Americans and South Koreans to settle their disputes. Apprised of the ROK intransigence and war fever, President Johnson wisely deferred to General Bonesteel and Ambassador Porter and sent an envoy immediately. Cyrus R. Vance arrived in Seoul on 10 February.

Vance possessed topflight credentials. A former secretary of the Army and deputy secretary of defense, Vance had spoken for Johnson and the United States in several delicate situations: Panama in January 1965; the Dominican Republic (that same year); in Detroit during the riots of June 1967; and on strife-torn Cyprus that autumn.[26] He would speak softly enough to the Koreans, but his words would be blunt.

As usual, Vance traveled light. Only John E. Walsh, ambassador to Kuwait, and translator Daniel A. O'Donoghue accompanied the troubleshooter. Bonesteel and Porter met the trio at the airport, and they took off immediately for the secure confines of U.S. Eighth Army headquarters. Walsh experienced a frigid flight in a bubble-topped, little OH-23 while perched unceremoniously on Bonesteel's lap. With the Blue House raiders just run to ground, even the commanding general could not afford to borrow one of the few enclosed UH-1 Hueys. The cold flight said a lot about the resource situation in United Nations Command. Bonesteel might have done it intentionally, to make a point.

Vance wanted to meet immediately with President Park, but ROK Blue House staffers rebuffed his request with uncharacteristic rudeness. The officials told Vance that Park was meeting with his military planners and not to be disturbed. Unable to arrange a meeting, and looking ahead to a banquet that evening sponsored by the ROK Army, Vance and his men huddled with Bonesteel and Porter. The fivesome went over some hundred discrete issues, ensuring a unified front. Vance would do all the talking for the next few days.

At the ROK Army dinner that night, the Americans stuck to light conversation and banal, obvious toasts. Their excited counterparts talked with conviction about the mighty things to come as the allies avenged the Blue House and *Pueblo* incidents. The southerners seemed to think that Vance's arrival presaged the great march north. One boozy ROK general cornered Ambassador Walsh and confided in him: "We're blood brothers.... When you are hurt, we are hurt."[27] If Vance and his partners had any doubts about ROK belligerence, the banquet demonstrated just how wild things had gotten in Seoul.

When Vance met Park the next day, the South Korean president proved quite obstinate. But Vance did not compromise. Johnson's spokesman laid out his position frankly. First, there would be no wider war in Korea—period; the U.S. already had its hands full in Vietnam. Any ROK military action against the north would be cleared with General Bonesteel, and he was not empowered to allow South Korean cross-border reprisals without President Johnson's approval. Vance made it clear that he could foresee no circumstances—short of a full-scale North Korean invasion—that could garner such approval.

Second, with a military attack ruled out, the United States would negotiate as necessary in order to gain freedom for the *Pueblo* sailors. Vance reminded Park that America had a tradition of talking with groups and states it did not recognize, including such thorns as the Barbary pirates, the Filipino insurgents, and Pancho Villa. This matter was between the United States and North Korea.

Finally, Vance offered some sweetener with the bitter gruel. He promised Park $100 million in immediate military aid, to include F-4 series Phantom fighter jets for the ROK Air Force; additional assistance would follow. To get this equipment, Park had to vow not to go north.

For four days, Park equivocated. But he really had no choice. Without the United States, South Korea could never hope to defeat the DPRK at any acceptable cost. The ROK leader finally consented to reign in his generals. Vance left, his mission accomplished. Presidents Johnson and Park met in Honolulu in April to seal the deal.[28] So the great crisis abated. A midintensity war had been averted. The low-intensity war, however, remained to be won.

## *The Conventional Response: Resources*

General Bonesteel made good use of the Blue House and *Pueblo* incidents to garner the additional visibility and funding he needed to throttle the North Korean unconventional threat. While careful not to divert resources from Vietnam, Bonesteel knew enough about bureaucratic politics to make sure that he received a priority on what was left over. He made his case both within the military establishment and among the larger community of American political leaders.

The general did his best to convince his military commanders and the military as an institution that Americans in Korea were in a real war. While U.S. Pacific Command agreed, the service departments and the Defense Department held the final authority. If they admitted that any part of Korea was a combat zone, that would formally give Bonesteel's theater a priority second only to Vietnam.[29] This formal recognition would help both American and South Korean morale and signal continued U.S. commitment to prevail in the Second Korean Conflict.

Due to the narrow prerogatives granted by operational control, Bonesteel could not do much to influence internal U.S. Air Force or U.S. Navy policies toward Korea. For the Navy and Air Force, Korea did not constitute combat. Both services, especially the U.S. Navy, wanted to reduce their post-*Pueblo* shows of force as soon as possible. Neither the Air Force nor the Navy moved to grant any sort of combat incentives to their deployed contingency forces, although airmen later benefited from Bonesteel's efforts.

Bonesteel wisely concentrated his efforts within his own U.S. Army. After all, by 1968, he could point to numerous patrolling and ambush casualties—all from the ranks of the U.S. Army. Obviously, whatever sailors and airmen might think, Korea was not just another overseas tour for soldiers.

Until 1968, Korea fell into an odd category with regard to combat pay and awards. In Korea, as in the Dominican Republic intervention of 1965–66, provisions already existed to give combat pay—but only to American dead (one month, paid posthumously, of course) and wounded (three months' pay or paid while hospitalized, whichever was shorter). If qualified by duty position and recommended by their division commanders, these casualties might also receive Combat Infantryman Badges or Combat Medical Badges.[30] Those not actually hit by hostile fire soldiered on, their sacrifices and dangers officially unrecognized. By the U.S. Army's reckoning, soldiers on patrol in the DMZ received the same official consideration as those in garrison at Fort Benning, Georgia.

Bonesteel changed that. Since mid-1967, the general had been pressuring the Department of the Army (as Commander, U.S. Eighth Army) and Department of Defense (as Commander, USFK and CINCUNC) for designation of the area north of the Imjin River and south of the DMZ's center (the Military Demarcation Line) as a "hostile fire zone." Soldiers and airmen serving or flying in this zone would receive hostile fire pay and other combat incentives. Only about 4,000 men would be involved, almost all from the U.S. 2d Infantry Division.

Before 1968, nobody at the Department of Defense really wanted to agree to such a move for fear of spurring the pugnacious ROKs to think that the United States was moving toward midintensity war. After the Blue House raid, the *Pueblo* incident, and the Vance visit, the South Koreans had been cowed. Designation of a hostile fire zone might serve to demonstrate that the United States recognized the Second Korean Conflict and stood by its ally. Keeping the zone discrete, however, would underscore the sharp limits to U.S. involvement.[31]

On 1 April 1968, largely at the insistence of outgoing Secretary McNamara, the Department of Defense announced that U.S. forces serving in or flying over the DMZ-Imjin sector would be given hostile fire pay. Army troops who spent six months in this area received an overseas service bar and the privilege to wear their combat organizational patch on their right sleeve for the remainder of their time in service. Within a few months, the commanding general of U.S. Eighth Army received permission to award the Combat Infantryman Badge and Combat Medical Badge to all qualified men serving north of the Imjin River.[32]

Bonesteel did not confine his promotional efforts to the military. He went out of his way to make the case for a stronger defense in Korea to interested civilian lawmakers, government executives, and influential private citizens. Bonesteel welcomed hundreds of visitors, even during the height of the 1968 crisis period. He explained the nature of what he termed the "porous war" on the peninsula and made it clear what he thought he needed to finish the job.[33]

As a result, both executive decision makers and Congress had access to informed opinions about what was necessary in Korea. Along with the $100 million in assistance to the ROKs promised by Cyrus Vance, Congress appropriated $230 million more to improve both U.S. and ROK facilities and combat readiness throughout the United Nations Command's Korean domain.[34] In light of legislative discontent with the Johnson administration in general, and the Vietnam War in particular, this reflected directly on Bonesteel's ability to make his argument heard.

Bonesteel's lobbying within the defense community and the American policy-making stratum opened the door to more resources—not a great amount, but enough. More important, these measures forced Bonesteel's superiors to acknowledge the Second Korean Conflict as a real war. "They are in every sense involved in combat," noted a Joint Chiefs of Staff memorandum.[35] To the extent allowed in his economy-of-force theater, Bonesteel now had the wherewithal to meet the DPRK challenge.

## The Unconventional Response: The DMZ

Bonesteel knew exactly what to do with his increased budget, thanks in large part to the detailed forecast prepared for the late 1967 Counterinfiltration-Guerrilla Concept Requirements Plan. Unfortunately, he did not control all of the funds. Since President Park had a major say in the spending priorities for the initial $100 million and the follow-on military assistance monies, Bonesteel could not direct the exact purchase patterns. On their part, Park and his generals succumbed to the attraction of purchasing eighteen new F-4D Phantom II aircraft—consuming well over one-third of the first $100 million.[36] Obtaining chain-link fencing, platoon radios, and night-vision devices amounted to small potatoes next to the gleaming promise of new fighter jets.

Bonesteel did what he could to influence the use of the remaining money, and he closely monitored those funds earmarked strictly for U.S. use. The general recognized that the window of opportunity opened by the troubles of early 1968 would not stay open forever, so he focused on those things most useful to his missions of DMZ counterinfiltration, sea approach counterinfiltration, and counterinsurgency.

Unwilling to count on appropriations from the ROKs and Washington, Bonesteel's logisticians took advantage of the general increase in stock permitted after the *Pueblo* capture. Rather than ordering vast quantities of ammunition and weapons, UNC supply planners requested a great many mundane counterinfiltration and counterguerrilla items for delivery by the massive USAF airlift that brought in the Combat Fox units. Thousands of

The F-4D Phantom II

tons of critical barrier materials and communications gear—worth some $32 million—arrived via the largest strategic airlift in history up to that time.[37] The UNC used these materials to complete the chain-link fence and its associated barrier defense system. By 30 July, the line spanned the entire south boundary of the DMZ, ready to detect infiltrators and delay their progress sufficiently for quick-reaction forces to finish them off.

The completion of the fence tied together the U.S.-ROK efforts along the DMZ. With physical linkup completed, Bonesteel took steps to extend the juncture into the combined command structure, a course foreshadowed by the consciously mixed Special Working Group of November 1966. Prior to late 1968, South Koreans served only as liaison officers on UNC and USFK staffs. In October, the U.S.-ROK Operational Planning Staff began work, specifically to deal with the anti-infiltration fight. The staff totaled only twenty-four men, seventeen of them Korean. Though more a cell than a true staff, this important conclave represented the first permanent and official ROK voice in the combined command.[38]

Along with supplies and a new combined planning organization, Bonesteel's UNC received one small but invaluable reinforcement unit: the U.S. 6th Combat Aviation Platoon, originally en route to Vietnam. This outfit's six UH-1D Hueys doubled the number of useful air-assault platforms in Korea. In conjunction with the six overworked Hueys on hand and the obsolescent OH-23 Ravens, the 6th Platoon finally gave the allies sufficient lift to maintain a ready heliborne quick-reaction force on strip alert, while at the same time employing some Hueys on neutralization operations. The platoon normally worked directly for I Corps (Group), although Bonesteel often saw fit to loan the platoon to the ROK Army for counterinsurgency missions in the interior.[39] The new combined staff made such transfers easier.

Aside from these welcome developments, the rest of the anti-infiltration improvements occurred only in the American sector. This made sense, because the Americans guarded the key avenues that headed toward Seoul, and these same Americans had failed so utterly to detect the Blue House raiders. For the sake of both tactical necessity and alliance politics, the U.S. sector had to be tightened up.

Manpower remained a problem, both in quantity and quality. The short-handed U.S. 2d Infantry Division could not send out enough patrols nor man enough positions to seal off its thirty-kilometer-long DMZ sector. The backup U.S. 7th Infantry Division, smaller than the 2d Division to start with, found itself stretched thin as it guarded various nuclear weapons sites, defended the U.S. Embassy in Seoul, and provided an on-call QRF for I Corps (Group).

The quantitative deficiencies proved easier to solve. Worried Department of the Army officials pumped a few thousand additional enlisted men into the Eighth Army replacement pipeline. They also authorized one-month tour extensions for certain key leaders and skilled troops in Korea, a policy rejected outright by the Air Force and Navy Departments.[40] Along with U.S. Eighth Army's prudent restrictions on leaves and passes and some tough internal cross-leveling of personnel, this erased the manpower deficit that plagued DMZ units before 1968.

Quality, of course, also had to be addressed. The U.S. Army tried to bolster the leadership situation in Korea, a tough proposition with Vietnam going full tilt. Bonesteel received a few more company-grade officers and sergeants with Vietnam experience, although not nearly enough to take charge of the rapidly swelling ranks of the infantry divisions. Shortages meant that inexperienced and incompetent leaders had to be used. It had always been a problem during Bonesteel's tour, but now the inept chiefs had more Indians to misuse. Without good leaders, more men provided little added combat punch.

With many lower-level leadership slots unfilled, the American forces resorted to their usual solutions: schools and supervision. Vigorous unit schooling in counterinfiltration tactics made trained leaders, if not sergeants, out of the more promising privates. The well-known "Imjin Scouts" patrol leaders' program dates from this period.

Greater supervision by higher headquarters ensured that the novice leaders did their jobs. Mindful of the strain on his field-grade commanders, Bonesteel moved a brigade headquarters from the U.S. 7th Infantry Division forward to the DMZ to take charge of two of the five battalions in the U.S. sector (see figure 9).[41] This reduced the span of control for the brigade commanders, permitting maximum influence by these experienced infantry colonels.

At the higher level, Bonesteel gained a subordinate general well suited to the unique demands of the Second Korean Conflict. The Department of the Army provided Lieutenant General William P. Yarborough to head I Corps (Group). A former commander of the Special Warfare School at Fort Bragg, North Carolina, Yarborough had pioneered many of the counter-insurgency concepts used by U.S. Special Forces.[42] He would be a useful source of ideas and leadership.

Finally, the U.S. Army provided three more potential combat multipliers. First, U.S. Eighth Army accepted a handful of bloodhound dog-tracker teams to aid in detecting penetrators south of the barrier fence. Second, soldiers received a few hundred precious M-16 automatic rifles, which for the first time gave those on patrol firepower equal to North Korean PPSh submachine guns and AK-47 assault rifles. Third, U.S. Pacific Command made two Special Forces teams temporarily available for use as anti-infiltration trainers.[43] Small things in themselves, each paid dividends when properly used. These DMZ improvements, especially the completion of the chain-link fence, the arrival of the additional Huey helicopters, and the adjustments in the American sector cemented the progress made the prior year. While the KPA attempted more infiltrations than in 1967, the allies were ready for them.

Thanks to better detection, contacts increased markedly, but successful North Korean penetrations dropped off. North Koreans began to fall victim to ambushes and suffer from chance encounters with alerted UNC troops. The KPA paid in blood for running the DMZ gauntlet, sustaining almost twice as many losses as in 1967.

The new UNC tactics worked. In a typical example on 19 September, outposts of the 3d Brigade, U.S. 2d Infantry Division, detected five northern intruders at the fence. The Americans, aided by their Korean Counter Agent Company, coordinated a dawn attack by an air-assault reaction force, armored cavalry, and mechanized infantry to isolate and eliminate the hostile team. A succession of similar efforts enabled U.S. 2d Infantry Division to claim that it had repulsed or killed twenty-five of twenty-seven agents between June and November, the height of the infiltration season.[44] ROK units enjoyed similar little victories. Win or lose, each skirmish made it just that much harder for the next KPA special unit to confront the steadily improving DMZ defenses.

**On the DMZ**

    ROK 99th Regimental Combat Team[1]
        1-99 Infantry
        2-99 Infantry
        3-99 Infantry
    4th Brigade, U.S. 2d Infantry Division[2]
        1-38 Infantry
        3-23 Infantry
    3d Brigade, U.S. 2d Infantry Division
        2-38 Infantry
        2-9 Infantry (Mechanized)
        3-32 Infantry[3]

**South of the Imjin River**

    2d Brigade, U.S. 2d Infantry Division
        1-9 Infantry
        2-23 Infantry (Mechanized)
        1-72 Armor
    1st Brigade, U.S. 2d Infantry Division
        1-23 Infantry
        2-72 Armor
    Division Reaction Force
        4-7 Cavalry
        Counter Agent Company

**Chorwon Valley**

    3d Brigade, U.S. 7th Infantry Division
        1-31 Infantry
        2-31 Infantry
        1-32 Infantry
        2-32 Infantry
    1st Brigade, U.S. 7th Infantry Division
        1-17 Infantry (Mechanized)
        2-17 Infantry (Mechanized)
        1-73 Armor
        2-10 Cavalry
            22d Royal Thai Company

[1]Under the operational control of the U.S. 2d Infantry Division.

[2]Actually, the 2d Brigade, U.S. 7th Infantry Division, under operational control of the U.S. 2d Infantry Division.

[3]From the U.S. 7th Infantry Division, under operational control of 3d Brigade, U.S. 2d Infantry Division.

Source: 2d ID, "Operational Report—Lessons Learned, Headquarters, 2d Infantry Division, Period Ending 30 April 1969 (U)," UNCLASSIFIED, Inclosure 1.

Figure 9. American maneuver battalion deployment as of 30 April 1969 (typical after 21 March 1968)

It had taken time, but the conventional U.S. and ROK infantrymen had regained a definite measure of control over South Korea's ground frontier. "Their record speaks for itself," said Major General Leland G. Cagwin of the U.S. 2d Infantry Division; "The other side is coming through the barrier with less frequency."[45] The DPRK was fast losing its ability to come by land.

Helicopters from the 6th Combat Aviation Platoon, U.S. I Corps, sweep through a valley in search of North Korean saboteurs

## *The Unconventional Response: The Sea Approaches*

Unlike the DMZ, South Korean seacoasts remained very vulnerable to enemy infiltration. Though some equipment upgrades occurred and the ROK Navy worked with both ROK and U.S. air units in neutralizing North Korean contacts, the lengthy coastlines still defied effective defense.

United States equipment transfers allowed for marginal improvements in the ROK Navy. Aided by advisers from U.S. Naval Forces, Korea, South Korean sailors accepted two new patrol escorts and an old destroyer into service. They also standardized their communications to allow for better links to the ROK Air Force, ROK Army, National Police, and intelligence agencies.[46]

The most spectacular sea triumph came on 21 August, when two ROK Navy destroyers joined in a Korean CIA-directed interception off Cheju Island. A KPN-KPA special warfare team had been lured to the area, enticed by the prospect of rescuing a top operative imprisoned on the island. ROK Air Force fighters and even USAF F-4 Phantoms flew cover during a running gunfight that ended with the North Korean craft sunk and its passengers killed or captured.[47]

The Cheju victory suggested the real problem with the game but overmatched ROK fleet. Lacking long-range patrol planes and coastal radars, the ROK Navy worked best after enemy intentions became obvious. The South Korean sailors could cut off sea reinforcements or catch known hostiles offshore—but only after being notified by landward ROK elements. Without a solid counterguerrilla net to snare them ashore, a great many spy boats could slip past the harried ROK Navy. This fact did not go unnoticed by the DPRK Reconnaissance Bureau, blocked on the DMZ and desperate for success.

## *The Unconventional Response: The Interior*

The Blue House raid caused President Park to make one important addition to his otherwise comprehensive counterinsurgency directive: Presidential Instruction #18. In mid-February, he finally approved creation of the Homeland Defense Reserve Force (HDRF), a popular militia. Formally announced in April, it proved to be the single most crucial step in the Second Korean Conflict.

Within 6 months, 2 million enthusiastic southern citizens, including 15,000 women, joined up. These formed more than 60,000 local-defense platoons and companies, formed around a backbone of former ROK soldiers.[48] While not well armed for some time, they became an invaluable information web and eventually a source of supplemental troops for regular ROK Army formations. It was the story of 1967's dutiful coast watchers in magnified form.

Emboldened and encouraged by the obvious attraction of the HDRF, Park took steps to extend the idea toward its logical conclusion by securing the whole of rural South Korea into the government fold. At the end of August, a scant month after the barrier fence had been finished, the first two of twenty planned "Reconstruction Villages" opened just south of the DMZ. Populated by armed ex-soldiers and their families on the model of Israeli border kibbutzim, these settlements created a band of fiercely loyal people squarely in the path of any likely northern infiltrators. Lone KPA intruders and small agent teams would not long survive in such a pro-ROK medium.

At the same time, the ROK Army reworked its old civic-action program. Formerly, ROK soldiers did civil engineering work, building roads and bridges during certain periods each year. The new approach put troops to work right in the villages to "promote ties between the military and civilian populace and intensify anti-communist spirit and support anti-espionage operations." The ROK units dug wells and built classrooms, clinics, and cultural centers. These community edifices could and did serve as gathering places for anti-Communist indoctrination classes.

The most important ROK civic-action effort entailed the dispatch of "Medical/Enlightenment Teams" into the forbidding, backward Taebaek and Chiri Mountains, scenes of much North Korean infiltration during the summer of 1967. These carefully schooled ROK regulars and reservists, in close coordination with the Korean CIA and National Police, conducted medical screenings, inoculations, and minor surgery. They also "enlightened" the local people by spreading the "gospel" according to Park Chung Hee, hoping also to inoculate the villagers against North Korean Communist propaganda. The teams met warm receptions.[49]

At this point, these efforts were still tentative and experimental. When they proved popular, Park went further. By the early 1970s, the rural information programs metamorphosed into the government-mandated *Saemaul* (New Community Movement) throughout the villages of the south. This rural mass movement squarely confronted Kim Il-sung's nationalistic *Juche* brand of communism. *Saemaul* offered a southern mixture of village cooperation, southern democratic tolerance (as versus northern "arrogance"), a sense of mission, and a pioneer spirit to raise rural production and living standards.[50] Park intended to challenge Kim Il-sung on all fronts, including ideology. The Reconstruction Villages, new ROK Army Civic Action Program, and Medical-Enlightenment Teams of 1968 merely became the first steps in the education of the countryside in proper ROK patriotism.

The special counterinsurgency units authorized in Presidential Instruction #18 also took shape throughout 1968. Much attention went to the reserve component ROK Second Army and its designated rear-area security divisions. Each division added a second counterinfiltration battalion. The Korean National Police continued to expand its paramilitary Combat Police, raising more local units that tied in with the militia below them and the supporting reserve divisions that backed them up. All formations received new American radios courtesy of the Combat Fox airlift.

The ROKs used the lull after the Blue House raid and U.S. air-sea buildup to organize and exercise these new units, to include training with I Corps (Group)'s new U.S. 6th Combat Aviation Platoon. ROK Army regulars and U.S. advisers designed and supervised the training, integrating selected, regular ROK forces as necessary.[51] By midsummer, after many field problems and a few small-scale call-ups, they seemed ready.

Even the Americans joined in the general enthusiasm for counterinsurgency. Notoriously ethnocentric and determined to speak English, the U.S. troops were ill-suited for village counterinsurgency work, as Bonesteel recognized. Still, an attempt had to be made to show that the American troops also cared about the Korean people and their problems. Some sort of cultural awareness and language familiarization might permit better working relationships with local people in the U.S. sector—not to mention better U.S.-ROK relations overall. In a struggle for hearts and minds, every little bit could help.

Previous U.S. efforts in this direction had been honored in the breach; an abortive 1966 2-week voluntary school fizzled after educating less than 200 U.S. 2d Infantry Division soldiers. To work, the new program would have to be mandatory and go beyond mere "welcome to Korea" classes. When an experimental version received positive feedback from participating units, Bonesteel and his subordinate commanders gave the idea command emphasis and implemented it.[52]

The consequent "Eighth US Army Education and Individual Action Program," or "Cold War Program" for short, was in place by late spring of 1968. It reached its full fruition under the watchful eye of counterguerrilla expert General Yarborough. Described as "a revolutionary program which consists of educational materials that actually change attitudes to a significant degree," the scheme endeavored to help U.S. troops "work and associate more constructively with Koreans." The KATUSA soldiers assigned to American companies played pivotal roles in the program, acting as conduits that connected the American soldiers with Korean villagers.

Along with sustaining classes and field trips, American troops took an active role in supporting Korean social welfare establishments. The U.S. 2d Infantry Division, for example, supported thirteen orphanages; taught English at fifteen nearby schools; conducted cultural exchanges with certain universities; and helped with an average of thirty local construction, medical, and educational projects. Division operational reports listed implementation of the EUSA Cold War Program as one of four missions, coequal to defense against conventional attack, counterinfiltration, and implementation of the 1953 Armistice Agreement.[53]

Did the Cold War Program make any difference? It is hard to say, but this much can be sure; it offered clear proof that U.S. troops were serious about their role as defenders of the ROK, not just occupiers. Given the torrent of North Korean propaganda that forever built on images of U.S. troops as whoring, drunken colonizers who ran over old people and abused children, the person-to-person contacts created by the Cold War Program certainly provided some strong evidence to the contrary.[54] In combination with the UNC's other steps, it certainly dealt more damage to DPRK credibility—an important matter in a struggle for popular loyalty.

The cumulative effects of the 1968 initiatives spelled disaster for North Korean underground networks throughout the south. Stunned by the Blue House raid, South Koreans rallied to the Park government, which moved quickly to set up new militia units, reconstruction villages, real civic-action projects, and medical-enlightenment teams to accommodate the popular ground swell.

Aided by thousands of willing informants, the Korean CIA cracked major spy rings in February, July, and August—bagging 132 key agents in the process. These DPRK networks had reached into the military, the police, the intelligence services, Seoul government circles, academe, religious groups, and the countryside. Some of those fingered worked as contract employees of U.S. Eighth Army, one of the cells having been in place since 1961.[55] But by August, they were gone.

The year that had started with such promise for Kim Il-sung and his generals had gone disastrously wrong. Shrewd U.S. diplomacy, ROK political pragmatism, and an intelligent use of new resources had made the DMZ untenable for the DPRK and enfeebled a big chunk of the North Korean intelligence apparatus. The only North Korean hope lay in a strike against the allies' weakest flank—the seacoast. It would be the northerners' last chance at victory.

## *The Ulchin-Samchok Landings*

Around midnight on 30 October, 120 men of the 124th Army Unit landed at 8 separate locations on the east coast of South Korea, between the towns of Samchok and Ulchin. The northerners had selected their landing beaches with great care along the boundary between two separate rear-area security divisions. After disembarking undetected from a variety of KPN clandestine watercraft, the men headed inland into the Taebaek Mountains for a planned thirty-day mission. Perhaps due to intelligence breakdowns, they did not know that this same area had hosted the Medical-Enlightenment Teams just months before, or maybe they knew it and did not care.

These elite 124th soldiers were functioning in their guerrilla organizing role. They intended to create long-lasting guerrilla bases in the south, complete with new informant nets to help make up for those wrecked during the summer. Any local officials foolish enough to intervene would be killed. As they reached their first objective villages around daybreak on 31 October, each of the eight teams rounded up the sleepy locals for introductory educational sessions. They had been told to expect jubilant welcomes as liberators. After some rote speeches and distribution of pictures of Kim Il-sung, the soldiers asked for volunteers to join the KWP. The South Koreans just stared back, dumbfounded.

In one hamlet near Ulchin, nervous 124th Army Unit members beat a man to death as an example to the others. That same detachment killed seven others, including a family of five, trying to terrorize the farmers into cooperation. Instead, even as the KPA special forces men filibustered and bullied, a teenage boy slipped a note to a woman, who in turn spirited the paper to her husband. He escaped unseen, running four miles to find a provincial police chief, who immediately radioed his superiors.[56] But they already knew about the 124th, thanks to many other reports.

ROK forces swarmed into the area. Some of the first arrived aboard the rotary-wing aircraft of the ubiquitous U.S. 6th Combat Aviation Platoon, summoned through the good offices of the new U.S.-ROK Operational Planning Staff. The American choppers joined six new ROK-operated Hueys, gifts of the American military assistance program. The 36th Rear Area Security Division, parts of two other divisions, an ROK Marine Corps battalion, numerous Combat Police companies, an ROK Special Forces Group, and thousands of Home Defense Reserves took part in the exhaustive manhunt that followed. Eventually, some 70,000 troops assisted in the operation.

Within two weeks, the elite, new ROK counterinfiltration battalions ran down most of the intruders. By 26 December, Park suspended the special counterguerrilla alert on the east coast. ROK forces announced that they had killed 110 and captured 7, as compared to 63 South Koreans dead, 23 of whom were civilians. The other southerners killed included regulars, reservist police, and militiamen.[57]

The ROKs conquered the North Koreans not only because of superior organization and some timely U.S. support but also because of strong local support in South Korea. Consequently, unlike the Blue House raid, the Ulchin-Samchok situation was never really in doubt. Thanks to thorough preparations, ROK forces "had the full support of the populace," General Bonesteel observed. "So," he continued, "it was a losing game to begin with for the North because of a miscomprehension of the situation in the south."[58]

Ulchin-Samchok provided the acid test for the United Nations Command. Pretty much on their own, the ROKs had prevailed against the best the north could offer. Two years earlier, the results might have been disastrous. But now, the ROKs knew what to do, and the Americans knew how to help them without doing it for them. Nobody realized it yet in the United Nations Command, but the Second Korean Conflict had been won.

# Isolated Provocations  4

> You know he's out there all the time just waiting for you to make a slip. It's a matter of pride to us to see that he doesn't get through.
>
> — an infantry private first class, U.S. 2d Infantry Division, late 1968

At about the same time ROK police, soldiers, and militia trapped and finished off the last of the Ulchin-Samchok landing forces, the North Koreans finally released the *Pueblo* crewmen. The United States representative at Panmunjom, Major General Gilbert H. Woodward, signed a DPRK-mandated confession of American perfidy in order to secure the final release. Once all eighty-two prisoners returned to UNC control on 23 December 1968, Woodward publicly repudiated the embarrassing statement of U.S. guilt.[1]

Yet to all appearances, the damage had been done. For almost a year, the mightiest power in the world consented to sheath its sword and beg for its sailors' freedom from Kim Il-sung's Democratic People's Republic of Korea. Kim had not missed a single chance to extract maximum propaganda value from the entire sorry affair. He mistreated the American captives, compelled them to record admissions and apologies for their imperialist "crimes," and then twisted the knife one more time with the Panmunjom confession—all the while blaring the tale of U.S. impotence to the listening world and especially into South Korea. One *Pueblo* sailor's taped lament played incessantly from banks of loudspeakers aimed across the DMZ at his countrymen.

The *Pueblo* seemed to symbolize faltering American resolve, an image reinforced by President Johnson's decision to curtail the U.S. war effort in Vietnam—not to mention domestic political assassinations, race riots, and campus upheavals. One Washington insider summarized the thinking among gloomy Johnson administration staffers: "The theory goes that the communists are determined to keep the U.S. humiliated as long as we stay in the Far East, and Korea is as good a place as any to keep up the humiliation."[2] The dishonorable nature of the *Pueblo* crew's return looked like the crowning blow to America's tottering prestige as a confident superpower.

Appearances can be deceiving, however. Even with the gush of propaganda triumphs afforded by the *Pueblo* episode, Kim Il-sung could hardly have been pleased with his overall strategic situation. His Communist benefactors, the USSR and China, were not only exchanging insults but bullets as well along their long common border. Kim could expect no big increases in aid from either power.[3]

This Communist bloc discord could not have flared up at a less opportune moment for the DPRK. This was a tough time for Kim Il-sung to be left on his own. After more than two years of intensive unconventional operations, the UNC allies had thwarted the best North Korean efforts. Economic and demographic trends, apparently unaffected by the northern offensive, continued to run as strongly as ever in favor of the ROK. Most distressing of all, the U.S.-ROK alliance had grown stronger, not weaker, despite some serious policy disputes early in the year. Kim held some American sailors and the headlines, but the United Nations Command held the initiative throughout the Republic of Korea.

Perhaps the DPRK gave back the *Pueblo* crewmen because they no longer served a purpose, other than as a possible casus belli for an increasingly more powerful U.S.-ROK military establishment. As long as the American prisoners remained in North Korea, they formed an unwelcome distraction from urgent political and military decisions facing the Pyongyang leadership. Its unconventional approach a shambles, North Korea needed new strategic thinking and a new set of officials to carry it out. While the public record offers only minimal insight into Kim Il-sung's logic, political developments in the north suggest that the desire to focus on cleaning house prompted the rather abrupt return of the *Pueblo* crew.

## *A Purge in Pyongyang*

Following the Ulchin-Samchok fiasco, Kim Il-sung wasted little time in junking his entire unconventional warfare campaign. A few days after the *Pueblo* crewmen departed, Kim's ax fell, taking out a wide swath of senior military officers closely associated with the prosecution of the Second Korean Conflict. Among others, these included defense minister, General Kim Chong-bong and his two brothers (both generals); KPA political bureau chairman, General Ho Pong-haek; chief of the general staff, General Choe Kwang; Reconnaissance Bureau chief, Lieutenant General Kim Chong-tae; KPN commander, Admiral Yu Chang-gon; KWP guerrilla activities secretary, Major General Cho Tong-chol; and the commanders of three frontline KPA corps. Kim Il-sung summarily executed Kim Chong-bong, Ho Pong-haek, and one corps commander—then promptly tossed the remainder into prison.[4]

The North Korean premier justified his harsh actions before his principal political and military lieutenants at the secret Fourth KWP-KPA Conference that convened in Pyongyang in January 1969. In a fulsome tirade, Kim Il-sung stated that the defrocked generals had "deliberately sabotaged" his campaign plan, wrecking it beyond reclamation. These traitors, he charged, "entirely overturned the military line of the party."[5] Kim elaborated on his accusations. First, the KPA leadership failed to translate the ideology of the Korean Workers' Party into a program palatable to South Korean farmers. Kim attributed this to the regular officers' lack of emphasis on developing committed Korean Workers' Party cadres in its special operations units.

This charge rings hollow, however, when one considers the extensive political education furnished to all northern special warfare units—particularly the elite, all-officer 124th and 283d Army Units. But by KWP logic, the political line could not be wrong, so the KPA's political indoctrination must have been faulty. Nobody dared to express the possibility that the KWP message did not appeal to the southerners.

Second, Kim stated that his generals neglected to make coordinated use of all of the assets made available by the much-touted "fortification of the entire country." For example, Kim noted that the generals never made use of all available ground, sea, and air assets, nor did they carefully coordinate those that they did employ. Most operations proceeded piecemeal.

The northern leader especially decried the commanders' unwillingness to rely on the extensive DPRK militia, which might have offered some help in integrating political agitation and military skills. He intimated that a dangerously misguided KPA distrust of peasant and worker political sentiments lay behind this calculated refusal to involve the Red Guards.

This charge held a bit more water, but only barely. While the generals often launched uncoordinated, high-risk missions, these mainly reflected Kim's own insistence on immediate, splashy results rather than the patient construction of a reliable southern infrastructure. The nature of missions was also affected by the limited number of high-quality special operators on hand at any one time. Any resort to throwing a great many conventional units into the fray promised little help in the unconventional effort and risked the big war that Kim did not yet want.

Even the premier's complaints about the failure of his generals to involve the militia seemed suspect. The generals understandably showed reluctance to use half-trained villagers in the volatile environs south of the DMZ, but they did not ignore these forces. The home defense outfits expanded in strength and received better arms throughout this period. This guard force served a vital function by securing the DPRK interior from ROK espionage and potential reprisals and thus freed regular North Korean troops for action.

KPA commanders employed the militia not only in routine uses but to validate unconventional warfare techniques. For example, the Reconnaissance Bureau tested its Blue House raiders against an entire battalion of specially selected Workers' and Peasants' Red Guards. The citizen-soldiers played the parts of ROK police and local civilians so energetically that thirty militiamen had to be hospitalized due to injuries sustained in these intense exercises.[6] This imaginative use of the DPRK militia did not impress the northern dictator, although Kim never made it clear just what he thought the part-time troops could add to his campaign in the south.

Finally, the premier observed that the purged generals never created a viable method for generating an insurgency in the South Korean mountains, even though the objective circumstances for building a guerrilla movement seemed to exist. Here, Kim argued that the failed leaders could not adapt KPA tactics and weapons to mountainous terrain, such as the Taebaek range.[7] This greatly concerned all North Korean officers. If even the cream of the DPRK's armed forces could not operate in the highlands, it implied a doctrinal failing of massive proportions for an army dedicated to war on a mountainous peninsula.

The tactical troubles in the up-country, of course, came from far more than any alleged inability to deal with the physical environment. Secure in their ideological cocoons, Kim and his cronies chose to ignore effective ROK counteractions and popular support and, instead, blamed the uniformed chain of command. The KWP line did not allow for any other possibilities.

Having fingered the culprits and their crimes, Kim Il-sung offered his new vision for the continuing struggle against the ROK and its U.S. allies. Kim used the same old catchphrase, "combining regular and irregular warfare," but went on to explain that this now meant something far different from what it had meant in October 1966. In January 1969, Kim argued that a combination of methods required strict subordination of all military activities to party goals. Just as the North Korean armed forces could only operate in support of KWP objectives, so special operations proceeded only in support of conventional operations—not vice versa, as had been the case since 1966.

With the military forcibly ejected from the subversion business, the premier transferred responsibility for creation of southern support back to the KWP Liaison Committee, which aimed to develop the moribund United Revolutionary Party as an actor in legal ROK politics.[8] Kim no longer gave much credence to the dream of fomenting a serious anti-ROK insurrection.

This new thinking resulted in crucial changes for the North Korean military establishment. Disgusted by his generals' mistakes, which he attributed to disloyalty, Kim Il-sung moved to ensure definite party control over every military activity. Kim instituted full dual command throughout his armed forces. Prior to this time, the KPA, KPAF, and KPN had enjoyed freedom from the onerous commissar system that deadened initiative in the Soviet and Chinese armed forces. After January 1969, however, every company-size element in the DPRK military received a political officer. These party watchdogs attended orders, rendered secret reports on their commander counterparts, passed on all officer promotions, conducted surprise inspections in accord with KWP guidance, and even held authority to shoot disobedient officers and men. No order was legitimate unless countersigned by a political officer.[9]

This major shift in policy hit the military quite hard. For twenty years, Kim Il-sung's officers enjoyed the favor of their former guerrilla comrade. When the party guardians arrived in unit garrisons, not all old-line commanders toed the line willingly. It took months to build a working commissar system, and further purges throughout the ranks were required to make it stick. As late as November 1970, Kim found it necessary to expel another slate of key generals as "anti-party factionalists" who "refused the military line" of the KWP.[10] He gained loyalty—but at the usual cost in innovative leadership.

Along with a thorough imposition of party discipline, North Korea carried out a complete overhaul of its special operations component to bring it into alignment with the more conventional approach now espoused. The infamous 124th Army Unit, the 17th Foot Reconnaissance Brigade (that so often worked the American sector of the DMZ), and the shadowy 283d Army Unit all disbanded. Each had lost too many key men in the ongoing conflict; the 124th had been particularly battered by the Ulchin-Samchok fighting. More telling, these forces had lost Kim Il-sung's confidence. Like the generals that spawned them, they had to go.

The dissolution of these elite forces signaled the reorientation of DPRK special warfare capabilities toward a role clearly subordinate to the conventional military. The remaining few thousand veteran special operators provided the backbone for new divisional light infantry battalions, corps light infantry and reconnaissance brigades, and a new national reservoir of chosen warriors called the 8th Special Purpose Corps. This distinctive corps included the amphibious arm and the germ of a paratrooper force, both soon to increase markedly. By 1970, these special units had expanded to 15,000 men, a solid start on the way to a current strength that by some estimates exceeds 100,000 troops.[11]

The new 8th Special Purpose Corps and its associates certainly gave North Korea a diverse and useful array of unique tactical units, to include more seaborne elements and a sorely needed air assault capability. Still, quality necessarily diminished as numbers went up. Good as they were, the refurbished and swollen ranks of airborne, naval infantry, mountain, and reconnaissance formations lacked the handpicked personnel, intensive training, and guerrilla-organizing expertise that characterized the rigorously schooled 124th Army Unit and its contemporaries. While they might complicate U.S.-ROK conventional defensive schemes, the DPRK's rebuilt special forces no longer could conduct an independent unconventional warfare campaign.

That squared nicely with the new approach from Pyongyang. Thanks to Kim's reinterpretation of his previous "combined warfare" idea, the DPRK returned to a hybrid of the policies of 1953—62 and those of 1962—66— conveniently couched in the now-familiar rhetoric of the Second Korean Conflict. As it had from 1953 to 1962, the north now put primary focus on reunification by overt conventional warfare, to be aided by selected commando missions that drew on the experience built up during the miscarried guerrilla campaign. Kim believed that his unimaginative generals had squandered a unique chance to undermine the ROK through special operations. With South Korean and American leaders now fully alerted to such efforts, the opportunity to create an insurgency had passed, perhaps for the foreseeable future.[12]

Yet the north did not completely abandon subversion. In line with the thinking of 1962–66, Kim also saw benefits in pursuing political erosion of the ROK, but only as an adjunct to invasion, not as a substitute. As in earlier times, the KWP would handle this undertaking.

The January purges, formal abandonment of the 1966 military campaign plan, and thorough reorganization of the armed forces, in general, and the special warfare units, in particular, created a window of vulnerability for the Democratic People's Republic of Korea. The revitalized United Nations Command forces definitely constituted a more formidable threat than they had in years. If for some reason the South Koreans or Americans chose to act, Kim Il-sung could well find himself in the same ugly quandary that his Soviet mentor, Joseph V. Stalin, faced in 1941: his army would be in confusion, his officer corps in disarray, and his allies distant and unwilling.

Thus, though the war was admittedly lost and the guilty already punished, Kim found it necessary to keep up a front of mystery and belligerence lest his cautious enemies discover too much and become bold. Leaning ever more heavily on his conventional units as his special operators underwent their painful mutations, Kim played his weak hand well enough to ward off any response from the uncertain UN Command. In the process, the North Koreans salvaged a few spiteful victories that marked the last year of the Second Korean Conflict.

## *The Allies at High Tide*

Premier Kim Il-sung had good reason to fear his opponents. The accumulated effects of over two years of American and South Korean political and military innovations reached their zenith by early 1969. The fact that this waxing power now served the active U.S. president, Richard M. Nixon, rather than the paralyzed, exhausted Lyndon Johnson could not have made the Pyongyang leadership sanguine about prospects for the coming campaign season.

Heartened by the resounding success in the Ulchin-Samchok operations, the United Nations Command put the finishing touches on the major programs of 1968. Anti-infiltration measures on the Demilitarized Zone and seacoasts dovetailed with the extensive counterinsurgency apparatus erected throughout the South Korean interior.

On the land frontier, both allies continued to improve on the tactics instituted during 1968. To aid detection, the Americans installed floodlights along a four-and-one-half-kilometer segment of their sector. Several UN divisions continued to test experimental electronic sensors of all types. American and South Korean military engineers and infantrymen worked throughout the winter to strengthen fortifications and clear fields of fire around the guard posts and the south barrier fence, all important to delay intrusive northerners. Most of the major construction had to wait until spring, but the allies did not allow weather to prevent routine position improvements.

President Richard M. Nixon, a new, tough U.S. president entered the scene against the North Koreans

Both the U.S. and ROK forces received delivery of a total of a dozen new UH-1 turbine helicopters. The Americans used these aircraft to enlarge their overtaxed 6th Aviation Platoon into the 239th Aviation Company (Assault Helicopter)—the first such Huey-equipped organization in Korea. The forward divisions located and readied numerous landing zones to allow better use of these new rotary-wing assets.[13] The additional helicopters and landing zones gave more mobility to the quick-reaction forces so vital for neutralization of infiltrators.

These ongoing upgrades, coupled with intensive training for U.S. and ROK DMZ units, made the zone extremely hazardous for the few North Korean intelligence agents and agitators who tried to take advantage of the winter ice, snow, and cutting, cold winds. Allied patrols and guard posts turned back several incursions without loss during January and February. One American after-action summary correctly attributed these achievements to the "vigilance" of enlisted men and "their quick reaction." The U.S. units still were filled with men brought in during the post-*Pueblo* buildup; though junior in rank, they were now veterans well-versed in the Korean environment. ROK divisions, always disciplined, also benefited from the extensive experience gained by all ranks during the bitter clashes of the previous year.[14] This new-found qualitative edge boded ill for the declining ranks of highly skilled KPA special forces, not to mention their unblooded conventional backups.

The UH-1 helicopter, used in Korea to provide quick-reaction forces greater mobility

With the DMZ so difficult, the northerners might have turned to the typically open seacoasts. These, however, no longer looked so inviting. In the wake of Ulchin-Samchok, new ROK Southern and Eastern Coast Security Commands had been established to oversee integration of everything from rare search aircraft to numerous citizen coast watchers. In this way, antiinfiltration measures along the barren shores benefited from the immediate command interest they sorely needed.

The emphasis on the beaches paid off almost immediately. Tipped off by sound intelligence work from the Korean CIA—carefully coordinated with police reports and air squadron sweeps—an ROK Navy patrol boat netted a North Korean spy boat on 25 February, the first of several intercepted and sunk during the year.[15] The exceptional cooperation of the year before became standard as 1969 went on. The South Koreans appeared to be serious about closing down coastal infiltration once and for all.

In the interior, the counterinsurgency programs continued to build upon the successes of 1968. The ROK Army drew upon their own potent special forces and activated two ranger brigades, each with five battalions. One went into the Taebaek Mountains, the other to the Chiri Mountains, the two usual havens for northern guerrilla troublemakers. These hard-bitten paratroopers, mostly veterans of previous fighting, retained the ability to relocate on short notice to anywhere within the republic.[16]

Intelligence efforts by the Korean CIA and ROK Army Counterintelligence Corps unearthed more DPRK sympathizers, informants, and deep-cover operatives. In one far-ranging escapade, ROK CIA men in Saigon nabbed a double agent en route to Cambodia.[17] In addition, local police, militiamen, and interested civilians brought in a steady stream of useful news and often participated in the final apprehension of enemy agents.

Finally, President Park's long-overdue conversion to the virtues of social mobilization proceeded full tilt into 1969. He increased funding for his formal Civic Action Program by 26 percent, with emphasis on the same sorts of medical services, educational work, and rural civil engineering that characterized the 1968 plan. As before, Park ordered his military commanders to concentrate upon "local community development and antiespionage operation areas."[18] Seoul's already strong control of the countryside would become ironclad in the absence of a viable North Korean guerrilla effort.

Curiously, with all the sweat devoted to the defense of the ROK against both midintensity and low-intensity challenges, neither General Bonesteel nor his intelligence staffers took any special notice of the significance of the wholesale changes in Pyongyang. But the general did know about the shuffle and even discussed it with visiting journalist Emerson Chapin early in 1969. Bonesteel correctly identified the affair as an inner-party struggle resulting from the reversals of 1968.[19]

From that point, though, the UN commander in chief's vaunted intuition faltered. Bonesteel did not think the personnel changes meant anything. He believed that the new defense minister, Ch'oe Hyon, had the reputation of being a guerrilla warfare specialist, which probably signaled business as usual. In a later public statement, the general went so far as to say: "The situation in 1969 reflects a north Korea ready and able to cause trouble, more so than at any time since 1953." Bonesteel thought that the noteworthy drop-off in North Korean infiltration merely reflected the success of continuing UNC initiatives, especially that of the new ROK Homeland Defense Reserve Force.[20] Perhaps better weather might bring about a resurgence of North Korean pressure, but the enemy seemed stymied by effective allied responses.

How did the astute Bonesteel miss the signs of real trouble in the northern military system? First, the Korean People's Army operational security proved to be airtight. If public sources and later actions offer a reliable guide, it took months before the UNC discerned the stand-down of the 124th Army Unit and its ilk—let alone the imposition of political officers throughout the North Korean command channels. The exact circumstances of the UNC discovery of these developments remain classified, but they probably could not be confirmed until well into 1970, after the Second Korean Conflict ended.[21] Without definite word, Bonesteel surmised that the drop-off in hostile infiltration corresponded only to UNC actions and not to any internal dynamics in North Korea.

Second, Bonesteel's favorite source, Kim Il-sung himself, remained rather tight-lipped and circumspect throughout 1969. As he confided to some scientific and educational workers in March, he found little time for detailed pronouncements because "the situation in the country was tense." His next major address on the South Korean issue came in November 1970, when he finally delineated his reversion to a conventional military program and renewed emphasis on the United Revolutionary Party as his front group in the south. The premier's few public statements in 1969 featured enough of the standard phraseology—"a burning desire to drive the U.S. imperialists from our soil and unify the country at the earliest possible date"—to convince Bonesteel that nothing had changed.[22]

But the great purge in January clearly indicated that something had changed—regardless of vague public statements. The 1966 change of plan had been characterized by a similar, though less extensive, purge. That time, the supreme leader himself spelled out his state's new direction. He had acted identically in 1950, 1958, and 1961–62. A new mass program, promulgated right from the top, followed every previous housecleaning.[23] This time, however, the cleansing lasted much longer. Though Kim already knew what he intended to do, he could not truly start his mass effort until the military had been restructured to his liking.

Given Kim's style of personal leadership, his lack of comment furnished sure proof that the DPRK wallowed in dire straits, caught in the interlude between concrete strategies. Bonesteel and his subordinates, burned too often by North Korean craftiness, chose not to read anything into this "dog that did not bark."

Aside from a dearth of hard intelligence and some faulty analysis, one should not discount the predispositions of the United Nations Command by early 1969. Almost all of the key commanders and staff officers recognized that the tide had turned in the Second Korean Conflict; even the cautious Bonesteel characterized the situation as "greatly improved." Justifiably pleased with the giant strides taken since the dark days of November 1966, the Americans and Koreans naturally attributed the dwindling infiltration rate strictly to growing allied tactical prowess. Few, if any, considered the possibility that allied success had caused a breakdown between Kim Il-sung and his armed forces and a consequent scaling back of unconventional operations at Pyongyang's direction.[24]

Solid intelligence on the real picture up north might have altered some of Bonesteel's perceptions. Even if he knew that North Korea was in trouble, the general's determination to avoid a wider war ruled out the kind of pre-emptive attack so feared by Kim Il-sung. More to the point, had he known what had gone wrong in the DPRK, Bonesteel might not have displayed so much optimism in his own troops' improved, but by no means unassailable, defensive abilities.

Without that knowledge, the Americans and South Koreans could only proceed from what they sensed—that the situation had changed greatly for the better. Bonesteel became so certain that things were winding down that he chose not to submit an expensive (more than $200 million) updated counterinfiltration and counterguerrilla requirements request to the Joint Chiefs, even though his staff had labored mightily to produce this revised document. He even authorized U.S. and ROK patrols to remark the DMZ's Military Demarcation Line for the first time since early 1967. Rather than deal with the northern threat, many of the U.S.-ROK senior staff officers instead prepared for the upcoming Exercise Focus Retina, a test of America's ability to reinforce its troops on the peninsula.[25]

Unaware of the North Korean plight and convinced that they were imposing their will on the conflict, the UN Command grew confident, even cocky. Inadvertently, they encouraged the nervous northerners to take harsh retribution.

## *The North Strikes Back*

Joint-Combined Exercise Focus Retina could not help but be noticed in Pyongyang. This mid-March war game featured the spectacular jump of a three-battalion brigade from the U.S. 82d Airborne Division. Tiers of light green parachutes blossomed in the late winter skies forty miles southeast of Seoul near the Han River. The Americans had flown thirty-one hours straight from Pope Air Force Base, North Carolina, intending "to demonstrate rapid reaction capability." Hundreds of jets from four U.S. Fifth Air Force tactical fighter wings provided notional ground support for the paratroopers (see figure 10). ROK special forces joined the airborne drop and the maneuvers that followed. The maneuver play included the repulse of a mythical aggressor that bore more than a passing resemblance to the DPRK. More than 7,000 troops (4,500 of which were U.S.-ROK forces based in Korea) participated in this impressive display of allied power.

From Kim Il-sung's vantage point, and according to his propaganda mills, Focus Retina looked like a dress rehearsal for the opening stages of a U.S.-ROK march to the north. Had the UNC figured out what was going on in the hobbled KPA? In any event, Focus Retina demanded a strong reply from the north. Kim's precise rationale for his response remains hidden in the bowels of the Pyongyang archives, but his reactions are definitely a matter of record. From March to May, the DPRK defended itself with a shield of blows reminiscent of the height of the 1967—68 skirmishing.

Korean People's Army regulars took the lead. They noticed that the U.S. troops had settled already into some complacent routines, and they used these patterns against the Americans. A few days before the U.S. airborne troops jumped, North Koreans ambushed a daylight barrier-fence repair

---

**U.S. Army from Fort Bragg, North Carolina (1,806 men parachuted in)**

    HQ, 2d Brigade, 82d Airborne Division
    1-325 Infantry (Airborne)
    3-325 Infantry (Airborne)
    1-319 Artillery (105-mm towed, Airborne)

**U.S. Air Force (approximately 300 aircraft)**

    18th Tactical Fighter Wing from Kadena AB, Okinawa
    347th Tactical Fighter Wing from Moody AFB, Georgia
    354th Tactical Fighter Wing from Myrtle Beach AFB, South Carolina
    475th Tactical Fighter Wing from Yokota AB, Japan
    Military Airlift Command airlifters from various bases

---

Figure 10. U.S. combat forces deployed for Exercise Focus Retina, March 1969

Part of the 7,000 troops participating in Exercise Focus Retina, a U.S.-ROK continental airborne assault exercise

patrol from the U.S. 38th Infantry—Company C of the 2d Battalion. The Americans escaped unscathed.

Two days later, on the eve of Exercise Focus Retina, the enemy tried a different method. In the full light of morning, a KPA guard post opened fire at long range against a demarcation-line marker-replacement patrol in the U.S. sector. One American died; two Americans and a KATUSA fell wounded. During a rescue attempt, these unfortunates died too, along with a pilot and four crewmen when the medical evacuation helicopter from the 337th Medical Company (Air Ambulance) crashed shortly after takeoff, a tragedy not caused by the enemy action.

The North Korean regulars probed U.S. defenses constantly over the next two weeks, but the wary Americans were on their guard by this time, and no further casualties resulted.[26] Sporadic clashes also flared along the ROK divisional fronts, to include a forty-minute firefight on 7 April. In this case, the northerners merely opened fire. Killing troops, not cutting through the zone, seemed to be their goal.

On the beaches, eight Communist seaborne raiders landed at Chumunjin in the Eastern Coast Security Command. Like their regular comrades on the DMZ, these operatives also showed little interest in subversion or spying.

Rather, the team seized and killed a hapless policeman, an act of terrorism repaid when ROK combat policemen and militia trapped and destroyed the KPA detachment.[27]

Obviously, when taken in concert with the virulent broadcasts and printed complaints blaring forth from the Communist media, these selective strikes served to demonstrate Kim Il-sung's concerns about Exercise Focus Retina. They did not signify renewed attempts to infiltrate South Korea and stir up the populace—a distinction not lost on Bonesteel. With Focus Retina over, there appeared to be no need to continue the cycle of violence on the borders. Thus, Bonesteel denied requests for reprisal raids by his frontline commanders and limited the UN counteractions to strenuous and largely effective defensive measures.[28]

Aware of the different intent of these recent attacks, Bonesteel tried diplomacy to curb the KPA. Perhaps the DPRK might choose to talk rather than fight. On 10 April, the UNC delegation at Panmunjom proposed a special meeting of the Military Armistice Commission aimed at reducing tensions along the DMZ. The impassive KPA general and his men heard the UN proposal and answered with four and one-half hours of stony silence.[29] So, there would be no succor from that quarter.

With the threat still looming and the North Koreans unwilling to acknowledge anything at the truce table, the Americans and South Koreans took precautions. Units assumed higher readiness postures along and behind the DMZ and in the exposed coastal command regions. Additionally, to emphasize that the war on the DMZ had not ended, the UNC suspended the recently restarted demarcation line marking efforts.[30] These activities would not resume until years after the Second Korean Conflict ended.

The North Koreans did respond to UN diplomacy—but not in the conference room and not along the DMZ. This time, Kim Il-sung's air commanders committed a calculated act of terror aimed to reopen the seams in the U.S.-ROK alliance. On 15 April, just after the northern premier's fifty-seventh birthday, two Korean People's Air Force MiG interceptors shot down a U.S. Navy EC-121M Constellation ninety-five miles off the east coast of the DPRK. The Communist fighter pilots issued no warning to the unarmed, four-engine turboprop, which lumbered along gathering electronic signals under a long-standing project code-named Beggar Shadow. Thirty-one Americans died in the one-sided encounter.[31]

The specter of the *Pueblo* seemed to be resurrected. This time, the evidence clearly showed a premeditated act by the north. There was little likelihood that some local commander had gotten bold given Kim's massive crackdown against his officer corps. Dare the United States and/or its Republic of Korean allies hit back?

President Nixon thought so. "We were being tested, and therefore force must be met with force," assumed the new U.S. leader. His national security adviser Henry Kissinger agreed. The president convened most of his National Security Council and weighed his options. Two USN carrier battle groups headed out into the Sea of Japan—just in case.³² Kissinger, noticeably excited to be facing his "first major crisis," prepared a slate of possible responses. These included a protest at Panmunjom, armed escort of future reconnaissance flights, seizure of North Korean vessels on the high seas, mining of Wonsan harbor, shore bombardment by air or ship gunnery, and retaliatory air strikes against the KPAF fighter airstrips. The president and his national security adviser agreed that only two options really seemed possible: a reprisal air strike or an aerial escort linked to a diplomatic complaint at the truce table. Both men favored the air attack.³³

But Nixon and Kissinger found themselves alone in their enthusiasm to bomb North Korea. Secretary of State William Rogers feared a public backlash from another military action in addition to the immensely unpopular Vietnam War. Secretary of Defense Melvin Laird warned that Congress would conduct its own retaliation, scuttling Nixon's other projects early in his administration. Laird also made the usual strategic argument: Korea was an economy-of-force theater, and anything used there diverted from the main effort in Vietnam. For his part, CIA chief, Richard Helms, also agreed that an air strike risked escalation and promised nothing but momentary gratification in the Oval Office.³⁴ All urged the president to limit his response to armed escorts and a note at Panmunjom.

The key men on the scene in Korea also warned against an air strike. Ambassador Porter recommended a mild response, for fear of encouraging radical elements in Pyongyang (or Seoul, for that matter). General Bonesteel also "didn't consider it wise" to react strongly, reported the JCS chairman, General Earle G. Wheeler. The general and ambassador cited intelligence sources, confirmed by CIA Director Helms, that indicated that the EC-121M downing was just another "isolated provocation," perhaps hoping to draw a UNC overreaction to suit some arcane internal needs in Pyongyang. So far, the ROKs had not stirred. Would they remain quiet if UN Navy fighter-bombers struck North Korea?³⁵

An EC-121M reconnaissance plane of the type shot down on 15 April by two MiGs

Henry Kissinger, national security adviser to President Nixon in 1969

Dismayed by the lack of support for their aggressive ideas, Nixon and Kissinger relented. On 18 April, the president announced that armed escorts would accompany future U.S. reconnaissance flights in the vicinity of North Korea. He also told the UN representative to the Military Armistice Commission to deliver what Nixon called "a very weak protest" to the DPRK general at Panmunjom.

In his mind, Nixon reserved the bombing option, but as the days passed, it became less and less likely. "I still agreed," wrote Nixon later, "that we had to act boldly. I just wasn't convinced that this was the time to do it." Like Johnson after the capture of the *Pueblo*, the president worried about launching aircraft and then finding himself at war in Korea. "As long as we were involved in Vietnam," concluded Nixon, "we simply did not have the resources or public support for another war in another place."[36]

The same factors that militated against a massive response to the taking of the *Pueblo* still restrained U.S. decision makers. Taking the long view came easier this time. The infiltration situation had improved greatly, the ROKs faced no special crisis, and the poor naval fliers were dead—not hostages. Thus, the Americans reacted to the loss of the EC-121M in three

Secretary of Defense Melvin Laird maintained that Korea was an economy-of-force theater

Secretary of State William Rogers, who feared a public reaction to intensified military action in Korea

A meeting of the Military Armistice Commission at Panmunjom

ways: the note at Panmunjom, armed escorts, and a naval show of force off the North Korean coast.

The "nonconfrontational" statement was accepted without comment by the KPA representative. The American delegation also withdrew until August to reinforce its protest.[37] The DPRK gave no indication of how it interpreted this missive, but it certainly must have calmed any invasion hysteria. Attacks on Americans tailed off drastically over the next few weeks.

The armed escorts proved easier to order than implement. Panicky Pentagon officials suspended all U.S. reconnaissance flights worldwide on 15 April, pending a decision on armed escorts. It took until 8 May to scrape up enough escort fighters to restart the missions. Given the heavy air commitment to Vietnam—to include the recent commencement of secret bombings in Cambodia—this should have surprised few. Nixon, however, raged against the "postponements, excuses, and delays." He might have been even more annoyed had he learned that Beggar Shadow flights had always received fighter escorts through the end of 1968 when requirements in Southeast Asia and the presumed easing situation in Korea encouraged a shift of these assets.[38] Once escorted flights resumed, no further reconnaissance aircraft were attacked. The KPAF declined to test the U.S. aviators.

In the Sea of Japan, the Seventh Fleet's Task Force 71 collected its warships and demonstrated its capabilities during maneuvers held on 19–26 April (see figure 11). Much like the Formation Star deployments of 1968, Rear Admiral Malcolm W. Cagle's ships conducted air and surface training—all the while reminding the North Koreans of the potential power lurking off their coasts.[39] Of all of the American reactions to the shooting down of the EC-121M, this probably carried the most weight. Four aircraft carriers with more than 350 warplanes could not be lightly dismissed in Pyongyang.

Nixon and Kissinger, however, were not happy with what the latter termed a "weak, indecisive, and disorganized" American effort in the case of the downed aircraft.[40] Yet together, these steps did the job. They mounted a credible threat, gave Kim Il-sung assurance that he was in no immediate danger, and, most important of all, maintained alliance solidarity. The North

---

Task Force 71 operations

- USS *Enterprise* (CVAN-65) with air wing
- USS *Ticonderoga* (CVA-14) with air wing
- USS *Ranger* (CVA-61) with air wing
- USS *Hornet* (CVS-12) with air wing
- USS *Chicago* (CG-11)
- USS *Oklahoma City* (CLG-5)
- USS *St. Paul* (CL-73)
- USS *Mahan* (DLG-11)
- USS *Dale* (DLG-19)
- USS *Sterrett* (DLG-31)
- USS *Lynde McCormick* (DDG-8)
- USS *Parsons* (DDG-33)
- USS *Radford* (DD-446)
- USS *John W. Weeks* (DD-701)
- USS *Lyman K. Swenson* (DD-729)
- USS *Gurke* (DD-783)
- USS *Richard B. Anderson* (DD-786)
- USS *Shelton* (DD-790)
- USS *Ernest G. Small* (DD-838)
- USS *Perry* (DD-844)
- USS *Tucker* (DD-875)
- USS *Meredith* (DD-890)
- USS *Davidson* (DE-1045)

*Abbreviations*

| | |
|---|---|
| CG | guided missile cruiser |
| CL | light cruiser |
| CLG | guided missile light cruiser |
| CVA | attack aircraft carrier |
| CVAN | nuclear-powered CVA |
| CVS | antisubmarine carrier |
| DD | destroyer |
| DLG | guided missile DD leader |
| DDG | guided missile destroyer |

Sources: Lieutenant D. L. Strole, United States Navy, and Lieutenant W. E. Dutcher, United States Naval Reserve, "Naval and Maritime Events, July 1968–December 1969," *United States Naval Institute Proceedings* 96 (May 1970):14; and Henry Kissinger, *White House Years* (Boston, MA: Little, Brown, and Co., 1979), 320.

---

Figure 11. The United States' response to the downing of the EC-121M, April 1969

Koreans throttled back. Incidents along the DMZ persisted into May, then died away in the U.S. sector, although the ROK DMZ divisions and the coasts continued to experience occasional incursions.[41]

## *The Torch Passes*

By avoiding contact with U.S. forces throughout most of the summer, the Korean People's Army achieved by inaction what it had never gained by fighting. With the Second Korean Conflict almost over, the "American imperialists" began to make long-term plans to pull out of the ROK (a process still in progress two decades later). The United States could contemplate this possibility because their South Korean allies had finally come of age—a development that more than balanced any comfort Kim Il-sung might have derived from waning U.S. interest.

In late July 1969, during a stopover at Guam following his visit with the crew of the Apollo 11 lunar landing mission, President Nixon told reporters that the United States would supply military hardware and advice, rather than U.S. ground troops, to support its allies. These allies could also count on American sea and air power. Though aimed at Vietnam, this "Nixon Doctrine" also extended to Korea. An alarmed Park Chung Hee flew to San Francisco in August to receive assurances that the U.S.-ROK alliance had not been altered. He accepted Nixon's word that basic U.S. policy remained intact.[42]

Yet despite these words, Park might have done better to look at what had begun to happen to his American defenders during the summer. With combat in the U.S. sector rare, the battle-experienced men brought in during 1968 were being replaced by novices. As one veteran U.S. colonel lamented, "a special kind of leadership is required to keep men 'up' during the lulls in enemy action."[43] Most of the time, the KPA did not cooperate by relieving the boredom. As in the rest of the U.S. Army about this time, troop quality, never too impressive in Korea to begin with, started on a long decline. Sloppy American soldiers suffered five deaths from accidental weapons discharges—equal to the number of U.S. ground troops lost all year to enemy action. Other careless troops sowed hundreds of little three-and-a-half-ounce M-14 "toe-popper" mines without regard for regulation marking procedures. More injuries resulted.[44]

Even the two remaining battlefield face-offs with the KPA sullied the U.S. soldiers' reputation for competence. On 17 August 1969, a 59th Aviation Company OH-23 pilot somehow became disoriented and flew his helicopter into North Korea, where he and his two cohorts quickly found themselves forced down and placed in custody.[45] Rumors of drug abuse swirled around the incident.

On 18 October, following months of absolute calm in the American sector, four U.S. soldiers from the U.S. 7th Infantry Division drove their jeep into the DMZ, trusting in a white flag to provide security. The North

Koreans pounced on the vehicle. Each American took a bullet through the head at close range, and their jeep was found riddled with holes torn by bullets and grenade fragments.[46] The lopsided skirmish suggested too many stark images from the ambush of 2 November 1966. It was as if the American infantrymen had learned nothing, but in reality, they were beginning to unlearn lessons that had been imparted earlier at great cost.

These developments of 1969 were just the first cracks. A year later, the same problems with drugs, race relations, and indiscipline that infected the forces in Vietnam had spread to Korea in a pronounced way. Things deteriorated so badly that a 1970 operational report prominently featured this ominous note: "The Assistant Chief of Staff G-2 has initiated a master list of all [U.S.] individuals who present a possible threat to distinguished visitors."[47]

Quantitative American contributions also started to erode. The air reservists brought to Korea during Operation Combat Fox left in June—unreplaced. Air Force aircraft strengths slowly drew down to pre-1968 levels. By November, the U.S. Department of Defense formalized the diversion of resources from the Korean theater. Due to a $38 million budget cut, U.S. Eighth Army laid off almost a tenth of its Korean labor force; deferred some military construction; and restricted usage of vehicles, spare parts, water, heating fuels, and electricity.[48] It marked the first outright resource reduction since November 1966. Once the cuts started, it was only a matter of time before the first big slash occurred: the withdrawal of the U.S. 7th Infantry Division in 1971.

While the Americans started down the slippery slope to a reduced force, the ROK military, its supporting agencies, and its faithful populace proceeded from victory to victory against the diminishing numbers of North Korean infiltrators. Between June and December 1969, ROK soldiers repelled numerous DMZ intrusions, trading mortar and even artillery fire with North Korean line units. On the coasts, joint air-sea-intelligence-police operations located and sank four 75-ton spy boats and captured another, the most impressive haul to date along the vulnerable beaches. In the interior, police and popular militia worked together to round up hundreds of agents, many reported by concerned citizens. Speeding into action in new helicopters, modernized warships, and screaming F-4D Phantom jets, the South Koreans had fulfilled Bonesteel's fondest hopes.[49] At long last, they could defend themselves against anything the north could throw at them.

Bonesteel himself departed on 1 October 1969, turning over command to Korean War hero General John H. Michaelis. It fell to Michaelis to negotiate the release of the unlucky helicopter crew. Their return on 3 December 1969 signified the end of the Second Korean Conflict, although intermittent small-scale DPRK-ROK scrapping persisted unabated well into 1971.

Michaelis pronounced the conflict's end in an article published in October 1970. "Continued activity by agents can be expected, but they should meet with no more success than in the past," he argued. "While north Korea might provoke incidents along the Demilitarized Zone, the probability of all-out hostilities in the foreseeable future is limited."[50] It remains so to this day.

# What Went Right

> In small wars, caution must be exercised, and instead of striving to generate the maximum power with forces available, the goal is to gain decisive results with the least application of force and the consequent minimum loss of life.
>
> —U.S. Marine Corps
> *Small Wars Manual*,
> 1940

Lately, it has become fashionable to refer to the Korean War of 1950–53 as "the forgotten war." Popular historian Clay Blair chose that apt phrase as the title of his monumental recent study of the war. If the Korean War, a three-year slugfest that cost America almost 34,000 battlefield dead, has been lost in the shuffle between the triumph of World War II and the trauma of Vietnam, is it any wonder that the confusing, sporadic, and far less bloody Second Korean Conflict has drifted into utter obscurity, blotted out by the awful spectacle of the contemporary war in Southeast Asia?

This studied indifference to an important small war is unfortunate given America's continued involvement on the Korean peninsula and today's constant soul-searching over the perils of low-intensity conflict. Military professionals and interested civilians would do well to consider the results achieved, the reasons for victory, the broader implications, and the unfinished business of the Second Korean Conflict.

## Decisive Results

By comparison to other wars, the human cost of the 1966–69 fighting in Korea appears rather small (see table 3). Including those killed, wounded, and captured in firefights and the *Pueblo* and EC-121M incidents, the allies lost 1,120 soldiers and police plus 171 South Korean civilians. Of this total, 374 troops and 80 civilians died.[1] To put these numbers in perspective, consider that U.S. casualties in Vietnam averaged more than 1,190 killed *per month* during 1968.[2]

## TABLE 3
### The Second Korean Conflict: A Statistical Summary, 1966—69

|  | 1966 | 1967 | 1968 | 1969 |
|---|---|---|---|---|
| **DMZ Incidents** | | | | |
| Firefight | 22 | 143 | 236 | 39 |
| KPA harassing fire | 3 | 5 | 19 | 4 |
| KPA mining | 0 | 16 | 8 | 0 |
| U.S.-ROK fire on suspected KPA | 12 | 280 | 223 | 24 |
| **Casualties** | | | | |
| KPA KIA | 13 | 126 | 233 | 25 |
| KPA WIA | | accurate totals not available | | |
| KPA PW | 1 | 4 | 4 | 3 |
| KPA defector | 17 | 10 | 5 | 1 |
| DPRK agents seized | 205 | 787 | 1,245 | 225 |
| ROK/U.S. KIA | 29/6 | 115/16 | 145/17[1] | 10/36[2] |
| ROK/U.S. WIA | 28/1 | 243/51 | 240/54 | 39/5 |
| ROK/U.S. PW | 0/0 | 0/0 | 0/82 | 0/3[3] |

[1]This column includes 1 U.S. KIA and 82 U.S. PWs (January—December 1968) from the USS *Pueblo*. The PWs were released by the DPRK.

[2]This total includes 31 U.S. KIA when their EC-121M was shot down by KPAF jets on 15 April 1969. It does not include 8 U.S. deaths resulting from the crash of a medical evacuation helicopter on 15 March 1969.

[3]These 3 U.S. Army helicopter crewmen were held from August until December 1969, then released.

Sources: Finley, *The US Military Experience in Korea*, 220; and Lieutenant Colonel Everett H. Webster, United States Air Force, "Is the Morning Calm About to Be Broken in Korea?" 8—9, Research report no. 4471, Air War College, Air University, Maxwell Air Force Base, AL, March 1971.

But there are other ways to consider these Korean numbers aside from the obvious fact that the soldiers were all just as dead, hurt, or captured as those lost on Omaha Beach. In retrospect, both the United States and the Republic of Korea can find some special significance in these sad tallies from three years of undeclared war on the peninsula. From the American point of view, the 319 casualties suffered during the 37 months of the Second Korean Conflict make this fighting the fourth most costly and second longest U.S. military undertaking since the end of World War II. Only the Korean and Vietnam Wars and the ill-fated Beirut expedition of the early 1980s took greater tolls, and only Vietnam lasted longer.[3] Although more widely reported and studied, the interventions in the Dominican Republic (1965—66), Grenada (1983), Panama (1989), and the Persian Gulf (1990—91) all proved less sanguine and much shorter.

For the South Koreans, this war cost 84 percent of all soldiers and 58 percent of all civilians lost to DPRK military actions since 1953.[4] To date, the Second Korean Conflict remains by far the single most violent period in the ongoing, smoldering postarmistice struggle between South Korea and the north. Only the original Korean War and the ROK contribution in Vietnam cost more southern lives.

What did the allies accomplish to justify these sacrifices? The military score sheet appears unimpressive at first glance. Given General Bonesteel's campaign plan, the U.S.-ROK forces did not achieve an especially favorable body count, killing only 397 KPA soldiers, capturing 12, and convincing 33 to defect. But again, numbers alone do not tell the full story. Almost every North Korean that fell was a highly trained special operator not easily replaced. Growing attrition among these few high-quality forces made North Korea's proinsurgent program markedly more difficult to implement as time went on.[5] Additionally, aggressive ROK internal security measures, especially the creation of the Homeland Defense Reserve Force in early 1968, netted a whopping 2,462 North Korean agents, informants, and collaborators.[6] Even allowing for President Park's tendency to toss domestic opponents into the bag of true DPRK auxiliaries, it still seems to be a huge haul. These damaging blows to the North Korean intelligence apparatus in the ROK evidently helped to convince Kim Il-sung that further unconventional efforts could not succeed.

Far more important than any body counts, the combined U.S.-ROK forces accomplished their mission. The Republic of Korea remained secure in 1969—and even stronger than in 1966. The allies' array of countermeasures derailed any realistic possibility for a Pyongyang-sponsored insurgency. Kim Il-sung had his chance, took it, and failed. After 1969, the south could turn its attention to the north's conventional threat, fairly certain that the DPRK had squandered its opportunity for an insurrection.

The frustration resultant from Kim Il-sung's attempts to stir up a potent guerrilla movement have had important and lasting effects on all three of the warring powers. Each involved state made major policy adjustments in the wake of the Second Korean Conflict.

For the ROKs, the victory of 1969 has proved both bright and dark. Success bequeathed the sort of yin-yang paradox so familiar to classical Korean philosophers. In this case, an uneasy tension arose between newfound economic muscle and internal repression. The issue persists to this day in the sometimes troubled southern republic.

The bright side of this relationship is the continued expansion of the ROK productive sectors, especially all varieties of industry. The United Nations Command shield provided sufficient security to permit a strong, populous ROK to grow almost unaffected by the northern provocations (see table 4). The positive trends that accelerated so dramatically in the late 1960s still go on. Thanks to the frustration of his 1966—69 schemes, Kim Il-sung today must confront his worst nightmare: a South Korea teeming with twice the population and four (nearly five) times the gross national product of its northern neighbor.[7] The military implications of this imbalance surely must cause the Pyongyang leadership to think twice before contemplating renewed war. This imbalance has created deterrence in the truest sense of the term.

Yet the drive to secure the ROK and protect its economic growth had a darker side. In essence, South Korea traded citizen rights for collective pro-

TABLE 4
Republic of Korea Population and Gross National Product,
1962–72

|      | Population (in millions) | Increase (in percent) | GNP (in billions) | Increase (in percent) |
|------|--------------------------|------------------------|-------------------|------------------------|
| 1962 | 26.2 | 2.7 | $2.3 | 3.1 |
| 1963 | 26.9 | 2.7 | $2.5 | 8.8 |
| 1964 | 27.7 | 2.9 | $2.7 | 8.6 |
| 1965 | 28.3 | 2.2 | $2.9 | 6.1 |
| 1966 | 28.9 | 2.1 | $3.2 | 12.4 |
| 1967 | 29.5 | 2.1 | $3.4 | 7.8 |
| 1968 | 30.1 | 2.0 | $3.8 | 12.6 |
| 1969 | 30.7 | 2.0 | $4.4 | 15.0 |
| 1970 | 31.3 | 1.9 | $4.7 | 7.9 |
| 1971 | 31.8 | 1.7 | $5.1 | 9.2 |
| 1972 | 32.4 | 1.9 | $5.6 | 7.0 |

Sources: Kim Mahn Je, *Korea's Economy: Past and Present* (Seoul, South Korea: Korea Development Institute, 1975), 342–43; and Frederica M. Bunge, ed., *South Korea, a Country Study*, Area handbook series (Washington, DC: United States Department of the Army, 1981), 56, 113.

tection. Although this guaranteed continued industrial progress, the ways in which President Park mobilized his people against the northern unconventional challenge left permanent scars on South Korean politics and society. Park apparently grew to enjoy the emergency powers he accumulated during the Second Korean Conflict, and he discovered that the same intelligence, police, military, militia, and social mobilization systems devised to defeat northern Communists also worked splendidly against domestic opponents—all conveniently cast by Park as "pro-northern agitators." In many ways, after 1969, the Seoul government replaced North Korea as the greatest danger to the average ROK citizen.

Even as the threat from the north receded, Park and his successors did not relinquish their powers. There were always enough sparks along the DMZ to justify further crackdowns. Labor groups, college students, and opposition politicians felt the unleashed power of the intrusive apparatus created to thwart Kim Il-sung's unconventional warriors. This resort to the rule of armed force, rather than law, produced a succession of tragic battles for authority in Seoul involving the military, the police, and the intelligence services. Stolen, illicit elections and a hastily rewritten authoritarian constitution led in a few turbulent years to President Park's death in 1979 at the hands of his own disgruntled Korean CIA chief. Coups, an army junta, and continued rule by a general-president have marked the period since Park's demise. Although there have been some promising moves toward real democracy, the military-dominated central government remains firmly in control.[8] Like the strength of the Samsung and Hyundai corporations, the overbearing might of the soldiery in Seoul is also a legacy of the Second Korean Conflict.

If the war delivered a mixed blessing to the ROK populace, the verdict north of the DMZ appears to have been much more clearly negative. The guerrilla option appeared to be permanently foreclosed, barring some unforeseeable collapse by the wary generals in the south. Worse, Kim Il-sung's vindictive purges had wiped out many key northern officers and burdened the previously innovative Korean People's Army with the strictures of a clumsy commissar system. Other than some experience in certain clandestine tactics, the DPRK gained nothing by its ambitious, unconventional campaign.

Faced with a much more capable ROK, today's sullen northern regime can only hold out and hope for a miracle to bring them any possibility of victory. Curiously, the overzealous ROK generals might inadvertently deliver that miracle by pursuing iron-fisted repression, thereby generating the deep-seated domestic discontent that Kim Il-sung's men had been unable to foment in 1966—69. But that is only a possibility—and not one that the north can control. If current tendencies hold up, the very survival of the DPRK will come into question within a few decades.[9]

The Americans, who suffered the least in the conflict, might have reaped the greatest benefit. Uncomfortable with long-term overseas troop commitments, the United States found itself able to begin a gradual disengagement from the Korean peninsula. This confident and virtually inevitable long good-bye began because of the excellent ROK showing in the Second Korean Conflict. The ROKs' prowess convinced the Nixon administration that it could withdraw an infantry division in 1971. That pullout was merely the first and largest. Throughout the 1970s, America made several incremental withdrawals, while simultaneously transferring more and more authority and responsibility to the Koreans through such vehicles as the U.S.-ROK Combined Forces Command (CFC) headquarters. The CFC was established in 1978 as the logical successor to Bonesteel's U.S.-ROK Operational Planning Staff of ten years earlier. Ample American high-technology arms, both granted and purchased, have been delivered to make sure that the southern forces maintain a qualitative edge on the North Koreans.[10]

Today, American ground units in Korea center around the U.S. 2d Infantry Division. The United States still maintains its formal command of all forces through the UNC and the new CFC. Given the ROK armed forces' deep involvement in domestic politics throughout the 1970s and 1980s, a relatively objective U.S. commander certainly helped keep defenses up while some of the Korean generals jousted for power in Seoul.

That American command, however, will probably change before the new century. Overall ROK command and final U.S. withdrawal are in the offing. General Bonesteel predicted as much as far back as 1970: "I can see a day where the U.S. forces in Korea will consist of a single armored cavalry regiment—a trip wire to hold up our end of the alliance. The ROKs will do the rest. That's exactly what we want, you know."[11]

In a sense, then, Kim Il-sung did achieve one of his goals, though hardly in the way he had hoped: the United States' forces will leave but turn over the fate of the peninsula to a powerful, militant South Korea. By then, the enfeebled North Korean leadership might decide that it prefers Yankee imperialism—if only as a brake to surging ROK ambitions.

## *Reasons for the Victory*

No one reason explains the U.S.-ROK victory in the Second Korean Conflict. Still, one could fairly argue that it largely derived from three causes: the flawed execution of the DPRK campaign plan, the UNC's ability to discern the northern threat and choose sound countermeasures, and the eventually comprehensive ROK reaction to the danger of an insurgency.

Like all wars, the 1966—69 Korean combat was lost as much as it was won. Kim Il-sung's unconventional campaign plan represented a superb concept poorly executed. In theory, the authoritarian, militarized ROK government, heavily dependent on a foreign power, should have been vulnerable to efforts to stir revolt. It was, but the northern soldiers botched their chance—probably for good.

The North Korean failure revolved around an inability to mass their special operations combat power against the objectives specified in Kim Il-sung's original blueprint. Lacking the proper numbers of trained cadres and without an established southern intelligence and logistics infrastructure, it would have taken the North Koreans years just to prepare the ground for generation of a viable insurrection in the ROK. But Premier Kim, fearful of the burgeoning southern power and cognizant of the diversion provided by Vietnam, refused to wait. He demanded immediate action, thus greatly hampering his armed forces' ability to accomplish the task.

Overly optimistic generals accepted this need for speed but ignored the consequent requirement (so well enunciated by Napoleon) to concentrate their resources before racing to battle.[12] Instead, they abetted Kim's grandiose guerrilla designs and sent their few half-prepared special warfare troops into action piecemeal within weeks of receiving their marching orders. The major forces built for the campaign (the 124th and 283d Army Units) were not even raised until four months after the incursions began and were not committed until fourteen months after the opening shots.

This haphazard commitment of forces resulted in fighting that lacked much discernible pattern and, therefore, much purpose. Rather than focusing initially on the Americans and widening potential clefts in the U.S.-ROK alliance, KPA special forces began to work directly upon the ROK population, thereby diluting their very limited strength between two formidable targets. All of this provided time for the UNC to figure out what was happening and devise countermeasures.

Individually outstanding achievements, such as the grimly efficient initial ambushes of November 1966, the precision demolition of a U.S. barracks in May 1967, and the near-miss at the Blue House in January 1968, exemplified both the great potential and the wasted effort of the DPRK campaign. Certainly, the north had the assets to brew up serious troubles for the UNC. But with the important exception of the Blue House raid, these skilled troops were frittered away against average U.S. riflemen, ordinary ROK soldiers, local police, and unlucky southern villagers—hardly the sort of high-value targets likely to unhinge South Korean society. With only a handful of special forces available, KPA leaders erred by not being more selective in their objectives.

Aside from taking little care in choosing tactical objectives, the infiltration teams rarely cooperated to deliver the sort of wide-ranging strikes and follow-up raids that might have paralyzed the UNC, particularly if such methods had been used from the outset. Rather, the whole northern campaign displayed an inexplicable lack of coordination. Forces did not move immediately to create or exploit opportunities like the Blue House raid, the *Pueblo* seizure, and the Tet Offensive in Vietnam; the DMZ and coasts remained quiet, and the squabbling allies enjoyed a breathing space to resolve their differences.

The only big, well-orchestrated North Korean operation, the Ulchin-Samchok landings, came several months after the allies had perfected a solid counterinsurgency structure. Even this massive infiltration attempt did not feature simultaneous pressures along the DMZ, thus permitting the Americans to shift valuable helicopters to support the ROK reaction forces.

One has the impression that the KPA commanders assumed that they might achieve something simply through "operating," by merely dispatching random teams into the south to prey on the Americans, ROK troops, and hapless citizens. All they gained for their troubles were steady attrition and increasingly more effective allied responses.

What if the North Korean leaders, most of them experienced in guerrilla warfare, had employed their forces differently? Although the brutal November 1966 ambushes offered immediate proof to Kim Il-sung that the military supported the new party line, they also tipped North Korea's hand. This led directly to UNC reactions that doomed the unconventional offensive. But it did not have to be that way. The northern forces could have saved their trained men for the decisive moment. It would have been possible to increase intelligence gathering without confronting and alarming U.S. and ROK troops or the disjointed ROK internal security agencies (which in 1966 posed little threat to clandestine infiltrators). By waiting a year or so as their agents shifted over from purely political agitation to setting the stage for dramatic decapitation raids, the north might have plotted a coordinated countrywide series of strikes against key ROK and UNC officials. An Ulchin-Samchok-size landing in the wake of such mayhem, against an unreformed UNC security system, might have produced far more drastic effects. Instead, the KPA generals settled for a series of small, immediate triumphs and lost the war.

As for the winners, victory came from properly identifying the problem and then taking appropriate action. General Bonesteel deserves special credit here. Almost single-handedly, as was his style, the cerebral general divined Kim Il-sung's new insurgency plan within days of its implementation. Bonesteel boldly challenged the standard beliefs of the U.S.-ROK intelligence staffs, who had hitherto watched almost exclusively for a repeat of the 1950 invasion. By accurately understanding the threat at the outset, Bonesteel spared his men a great deal of bloody, unproductive fumbling around. From the start, the UNC forces knew what they were up against.

Within a few months after heightened hostilities began, Bonesteel's Special Working Group of handpicked U.S. and ROK officers created the UNC campaign plan that defeated Kim Il-sung's proinsurgent activities. Guided by Bonesteel and ever aware that the United States could not fight a major war in Korea, the Special Working Group ignored America's "go it alone" ethnocentric tradition and reposed trust in the ROKs right from the start. The ROKs' ability to secure their own populace would constitute success. The UNC, mostly ROKs, handled the anti-infiltration fighting on the DMZ and coasts, leaving the counterinsurgent war inside South Korea almost exclusively to the ROK government.

Ignoring almost all printed doctrine and contemporary field practice, Bonesteel refused to commit his American battalions as mobile counterguerrilla strike forces. Instead, he chained them to the unglamorous but important DMZ security mission and greatly curtailed their use of firepower. This encouraged the relatively well-equipped U.S. troops to conduct some important experimentation to formulate the right mix of barriers and small-unit tactics needed to interfere with DMZ intruders. These techniques then became standard for the ROK soldiers as well. The DMZ service accorded closely with conventional U.S. tactics, severely limited any escalation of the American role, and threw the bulk of the war effort on the ROKs. Each of these expedients reinforced Bonesteel's favored concept of operations.

As Bonesteel envisioned it, the counterinsurgent war proper fell to the Republic of Korea. Whatever his eventual shortcomings as a corrupt autocrat, President Park Chung Hee distinguished himself in his conduct of the Second Korean Conflict. Early on, Park accepted Bonesteel's evaluation of the threat and consequently agreed to most of Bonesteel's suggestions. The ROK leader believed that, if carried out, these measures could accentuate the nationalism and guarantee the sovereignty of South Korea that Park so much wanted.

Park's actions are especially noteworthy because of the personal risks he accepted. Presidential Instruction #18, which created the effective framework for ROK counterguerrilla operations, tempted fate by requiring the suspicious fiefdoms of the ROK military, police, and intelligence services to surrender their independence to a definite chain of command. As these agencies could make or break Park (and finally did break him), this reorganization represented a substantial political gamble on his part. Had the Blue House raid and Ulchin-Samchok landings not occurred to validate the new policy, Park could well have felt a backlash from his offended, powerful subordinates.

In the same way, the February 1968 decision that formed the Homeland Defense Reserve Force represented an uncharacteristic trust in the average South Korean, the same people (in Park's mind, at least) who rioted in the cities and chafed under Park's political programs. For a man elevated to authority as a result of the chaos created by popular unrest, the choice to arm his people, especially in the face of determined Communist agitation, seemed like a very big leap of faith. The new militia might take their weapons and turn on Park. But like the powerful bureaucracies, the ROK citizenry rallied to their president in the teeth of the guerrilla challenge. In Bonesteel's opinion, "I think this [the militia] is what finally turned off the north."[13]

It would be wrong to suggest that the UNC did not make mistakes—including some serious ones. For all his brilliance, Bonesteel appears to have missed the significance of the KPA purge of early 1969, and his knee-jerk recommendation for a nuclear reaction to the *Pueblo*'s capture hardly did him credit as a sensible strategist. As for Park, he was slow to institute all of the recommended changes in his counterguerrilla apparatus and never bothered to deliver the political freedoms that could have cemented ROK society more firmly to its leadership. Finally, both the Americans and the South Koreans, despite their potentially substantial naval capabilities, virtually ceded the ROK coastline to the intruders. Although the Ulchin-Samchok forces failed, the fact that they could land in such numbers so late in the conflict says a lot about UNC shortcomings on the sea frontiers.

All of these mistakes hurt the allied effort, but North Korea's grave errors and the UNC's many sound methods counted for more in the final analysis. It is interesting to observe that in this most political type of war, the politically astute General Bonesteel proved able to impose his will on those most political of soldiers—General Park of the south and Marshal Kim of the north. More than any other individual, Bonesteel dominated the Second Korean Conflict. Its outcome bears his indelible stamp.

## *The Broader Implications*

Obviously, all participants learned, or could have learned, from their experiences in the 1966—69 Korean combat. For the Koreans, this knowledge may be of direct utility in future confrontations on their divided peninsula. As citizens of a global superpower, however, Americans do not have the luxury of focusing their attention in one place. Did the experiences of 1966—69 produce any insights that might be applied outside the Korean context?

It would be easy to dismiss the Korean case as unique and thus unworthy of serious consideration. Certainly, Korea features three elements distinct from the usual formula for American interventions in the Third World. First, the ROK in 1966 constituted a somewhat developed polity, with a growing economy and some social cohesion. Second, the United States had made a long-term commitment to ROK security, formalized by a tested wartime alliance, a treaty, and forward deployment of U.S. troops. Third, thanks to the continuation of wartime arrangements, the U.S. military command structure permitted the U.S. commander in chief in Korea to work around the U.S. embassy and exert operational control over the host country's armed forces. Many might suggest that these circumstances are so peculiar to Korea as to render suspect any general observations about U.S. actions undertaken in that country and their broader application.

On closer appraisal, the situation in Korea in 1966—69 was not so unusual. First, the ROK had the potential to be a stable sovereign state, but it also suffered from all of the expected pains of rapid industrialization, including significant political unrest and social dislocation. Add to this a semimilitarized government of questionable legitimacy and an aggressive northern neighbor, and it is easy to see that the ROK was vulnerable to infiltration and insurgency—especially if the government overreacted with heavy, indiscriminate force. Although obviously stronger than the Republic of Vietnam, the ROK was by no means a stable state fourteen years after the Korean War. One must be careful not to project too much of modern South Korea onto its 1960s predecessor.

As for the long-term U.S. commitment, this again is not unheard of. Like any world power, America has posted its forces overseas in many places, not all of them safe. One can posit a few fairly parallel cases, like Panama, the Philippines, Honduras, and El Salvador, where the United States has backed up its words with men on the ground.

It is also important to note that commitments made can be broken—regardless of the amount of blood and treasure invested. Lebanon, Iran, pre-1979 Nicaragua, and of course South Vietnam serve as pointed reminders that even long-term arrangements do not last forever. Had Korea gone sour, the United States might well have pulled out precipitately.

Korea in the 1960s was unique in one sense. The command relationships obviously seemed optimum from an American military perspective. Thanks to enduring Korean War practices, the theater commander in chief could circumvent the cumbersome ambassadorial "country team," a definite advantage in this case, although not completely unprecedented for U.S. field commanders.[14] The really unusual aspect of the Korean command framework involved the U.S. commander in chief's operational command of the South Korean military. Most countries, and even a good portion of today's ROK population, see such a U.S.-dominant arrangement as a violation of their sovereignty. There are some similar cases of agreed-upon U.S. command of multinational forces, such as the Sinai peacekeeping contingent or the Grenada intervention forces. But these sorts of structures are becoming less likely. More typical is a sort of combined committee, as in the American-British World War II setup. Americans found themselves in such committee war efforts in Vietnam, in Beirut (1982—84), and in the Persian Gulf (1987—88 and 1990—91).[15]

Even allowing for General Bonesteel's unusual degree of authority in Korea, it should be noted that U.S. operational control had definite limits. These were generally understood to relate to troop movements involved with prevention or conduct of a conventional war, which was not the major problem in 1966—69. Bonesteel and his U.S. ambassador counterparts could not and did not command Park Chung Hee, and the ROK president's decisions to reorganize his counterguerrilla forces and establish a militia proved to be absolutely crucial. Though Bonesteel could direct matters to some extent, he found it more expedient to persuade the South Koreans. In this regard, the command relationship in Korea resembles many likely Third World arenas.

In general, Korea is only unique in as much as all countries and all wars are unique. Having said that, the real question emerges: what are the broader implications of the Second Korean Conflict? Six come to mind.

First, *victory in low-intensity conflict does not always look the same as victory in a larger war*. Based on the outcome of the balance of individual engagements, the North Koreans could claim to have won the Second Korean Conflict. The UNC looked uncomfortably passive in the face of numerous small reverses—not to mention the alarming Blue House raid, the embarrassing *Pueblo* episode, and the unexpected EC-121M downing. Yet because the war revolved around securing the ROK—not matching the north tit for tat—these DPRK tactical successes meant little. In low-intensity conflict, a commander must keep his eye on the objective and suppress his conventional instincts about winning and losing.

General Bonesteel's decision to track enemy infiltration activity rather than enemy bodies exemplifies the different mind-set required.[16] The UNC tactics for forestalling infiltration rested more on allied defensive layers and ROK social mobilization than steel applied to targets. Making infiltration too hard to accomplish proved more effective, in the long term, than trying to locate and kill every intruder with armed force. In a war to protect unarmed people, the less violence, the better.

Second, *low-intensity conflict should be a combined and joint effort*. While this seems obvious today, it is an assertion more often spoken than accomplished. General Bonesteel took full advantage of the combined UNC force structure throughout his campaign and looked for opportunities to place more responsibility on the ROKs. He also employed those U.S. and ROK joint assets he had available to assist his war effort and showed the South Koreans how to integrate their nonmilitary agencies into the struggle.

Interestingly, cooperation in the combined realm exceeded that in the joint domain. Even at the height of the 1968 crisis, Bonesteel never exercised command over the U.S. Seventh Fleet or the U.S. Fifth Air Force. The U.S. Air Force, especially in the 1968 show of force, provided good support to the UNC despite the separated command structure. This reflected the joint interoperability built through the hard work of Bonesteel's private air arm, the 314th Air Division.

Unfortunately, the U.S. Navy missed a chance to furnish similar support. Busy with blue-water operations worldwide and brown-water fighting in Southeast Asia, the U.S. Navy provided little beyond advice (and not so much of that) to meet Bonesteel's formidable coastal defense problems. The U.S. Coast Guard, which might have been especially helpful, did not participate at all.

*The United States will normally be in an economy-of-force role in LIC.* That is one of the key traits that makes such a war "low intensity" from the American viewpoint. Economy of force means that the U.S. commander must work with what he has in theater. Bonesteel, aided by his U.S. and ROK subordinates, demonstrated an uncanny ability to make the best of available resources. A shrewd commander like Bonesteel will make a virtue of necessity. The restraints on American commitments can be employed to justify shifting the responsibility for wars onto the host countries. The alternative, Americanizing the war, is at best a short-term solution that can develop unhealthy dependencies in the host state and play right into the hands of nationalist opposition factions, to include insurgent groups.

In his insistence on a severely restricted U.S. role, Bonesteel deviated sharply from a prevalent American attitude of his time—epitomized by General Westmoreland's thoroughly "Made in USA" campaign in Vietnam. Today, American doctrine and practice come down firmly in support of the Bonesteel approach. The officers responsible for military assistance in El Salvador agree that "imposing some sort of ceiling [on U.S. participation] is a *good* idea" [emphasis in original] because it "preclude[s] any possibility of Americanizing the war."[17] In the overall scheme of U.S. security policy, a successful American effort in low-intensity conflict should remain at that intensity.

Not suprisingly, *small wars do not neatly adhere to the doctrinal LIC categories of operations.* Contemporary doctrine separates LIC into insurgency/counterinsurgency, the combating of terrorism, peacekeeping, and peacetime contingencies. Examination of the Second Korean Conflict suggests that the clear delineations described in today's doctrine do not really hold up in the field. The current FM 100-20 notes that "LIC operations may involve two or more of these categories" and that knowing how to handle each type of operation might allow a commander to "establish priorities in actual situations."[18] This is the only acknowledgment that things could get confusing out in the bush.

The doctrine writers go on to explain their categories, recommending certain discrete forces and tactics to meet *each* sort of LIC situation. For instance, the authors discourage any employment of U.S. conventional combat forces in a counterinsurgency, while noting that American conventional fighting units play a major role in a contingency mission, such as the evacuation of U.S. citizens from a hostile country.[19] That is fine advice as long as the situations remain clearly in one category or the other.

But what if a U.S. commander finds himself stuck with *both* situations? Then, current doctrine stands mute on what to do. Nowhere does FM

100-20 discuss the messy realities that confronted Bonesteel in Korea and faced other Americans in Lebanon, the Dominican Republic, Grenada, and Panama, to name a few examples. If only LIC operations adapted themselves to such a neat taxonomy!

Instead, the categories intertwine and become blurred. In Korea by March 1968, the UNC was faced by a simultaneous counterinsurgency threat in the ROK interior, cross-border terrorism, and a contingency show of air and naval force—all under the peacekeeping restraints imposed by the 1953 armistice. Just to further muddy the waters, one might mention the enduring menace of a North Korean conventional invasion. A modern professional would find it frustrating indeed to try to apply current U.S. doctrine to this all too typical LIC mosaic.

Since the doctrine of Bonesteel's era made no attempt to address this confusing array of dangers, the general met the challenges as he thought best. Then again, so did General Westmoreland in Vietnam. Rather than rely on the local American commander to act and then hope for the best, however, one would think that today's doctrine should accept and address the likelihood that handy theoretical categories rarely occur in nature.

*U.S. conventional combat units do have a role in counterinsurgency—if used wisely.* There is little doubt that, despite shortcomings and mistakes, the American forces of UNC contributed significantly to the allied victory won principally by the South Koreans. But stung by the bitter memories of the frustrating Vietnam experiences suffered by U.S. troops, today's doctrine all but rules out any use of American line units in battling insurgents.[20]

The Second Korean Conflict compels some reevaluation of that idea. There is a sensible middle ground between an Americanized counterguerrilla war and a completely indigenous effort supported by a few U.S. advisers and supply clerks. Bonesteel's UNC found two very effective uses for American combat troops from 1966 to 1969.

First and foremost, Americans in battle served an important political function by demonstrating U.S. solidarity with their ROK allies. This showed that the Americans were carrying their part of the war and thereby permitted Bonesteel to argue with President Park as a cocombatant rather than an uninvolved, and therefore suspect, foreign adviser. Bonesteel gained some moral authority, and he used it.

Second, Americans helped block DMZ infiltration along the major approaches to Seoul—an important and perilous role that made good use of conventional U.S. tactics. In carrying out this task, Bonesteel's men developed their own anti-infiltration doctrine, melding manpower, barriers, and techniques to find, slow, and finish off intruders. The American experiments became standard across the DMZ and remain so. Echoes of this innovative effort persist in today's LIC doctrine.[21]

Bonesteel's conventional troops contributed to his mission because he let them do just enough to help, without allowing them to plunge headlong into the South Korean counterinsurgent fight. It is probable that tying the

U.S. soldiers into static defensive positions and denying them any use of massed firepower exacted an additional price in American blood. But these measures also prevented escalation and made the ROKs carry the ball—two key ingredients in the UNC victory.

Lastly, *command in LIC goes well beyond killing the enemy and effecting destruction of his resources.* Senior commanders in LIC should be proconsuls, not Pattons (although that general showed some proconsular skills himself in French Morocco). Commanders need to be aware of American foreign policy, their place in overall U.S. strategy, host-country domestic politics, and adversary politics and goals. They also should understand where their forces fit into this complex situation. Without fail, they should recognize that they are in a LIC environment, not World War II.

Once alert to their surroundings, commanders should be as clear as possible about defining and pursuing American and allied political objectives. Good LIC generals "must adopt courses of action that legally support those objectives even if the courses of action appear to be unorthodox or outside what traditional doctrine had contemplated."[22]

General Bonesteel provides an intriguing model for a LIC commander. Intellectually gifted in his own right, conditioned by previous assignments to consider political factors, and unfettered by any excessive allegiance to U.S. Army tactical doctrine, he successfully recognized and met the challenges of the Second Korean Conflict. More a politician and bureaucratic infighter than a field commander, Bonesteel nevertheless concocted and pursued an operational vision well suited to the situation in Korea.

Bonesteel was not much of a troop leader, nor did he feel close to his men. Those tendencies, normally unwelcome in generals, probably worked to Bonesteel's advantage in his small war. He did not worry overly about employing his men in ways that they found disagreeable and confining; when they complained, he ignored them and stuck to his campaign vision. A more soldier-oriented general, a "warrior," might have reacted differently. Such a general might have employed his American troops more aggressively, ordered greater use of firepower to protect his men, demanded the right of cross-DMZ reprisals, or keyed on killing North Koreans. While such a tack might be better for U.S. soldiers' morale than Bonesteel's restrained methods, a more traditional American approach promised a weaker ROK or a wider war—neither acceptable results.

Every war, big or small, requires fighting leaders of high caliber. Low-intensity conflict puts a premium on a hybrid political-military authority at the decision-making pinnacle. The narrowly focused combat commander still has his important place, but the Second Korean Conflict suggests that he does not belong at the very top.

## Unfinished Business

The dwindling infiltration rate of late 1969 marked the end of North Korea's stand-alone unconventional campaign to subvert the south. It did not, however, signal the conclusion of all hostilities on the embattled peninsula. Military theorist Carl von Clausewitz writes that "even the ultimate outcome of a war is not always to be regarded as final."[23] Considering that the conclusion of the Second Korean Conflict simply restored the two Koreas to the uneasy peace created by the 1953 armistice, Clausewitz' caution certainly applies.

Occasional skirmishing, sometimes lethal, still occurs along the DMZ, the South Korean coasts, and inside the ROK. America has sustained casualties in this ongoing struggle, although never on the scale of 1966—69 (see figure 12). The South Koreans, as in earlier times, bear the brunt of this desultory probing. Although foiled in their bid to create a southern guerrilla base, Kim Il-sung and his generals continue to harass the ROK with a view toward creating some sort of opening for conventional exploitation. Kim's advancing age, coupled with the increasingly pro-ROK correlation of demographic and economic power on the peninsula, argues that some sort of northern desperation offensive is not out of the question.

Extensive North Korean tunneling under the DMZ, unsuccessful assassination attempts against President Park (1974) and President Chun Doo Hwan (1983), and a steady trickle of infiltrating agents offer proof of an enduring DPRK threat.[24] Even allowing for likely ROK exaggerations, these events, plus rumors of DPRK nuclear technology and confirmed chemical and ballistic missile stocks, require the U.S.-ROK forces to stay ready.[25] This dangerous situation has not been altered by the advent of Mikhail Gorbachev's reforms in the Soviet Union. There has been no corresponding *glasnost* in Pyongyang.

American troops will probably continue to pull out in bits and pieces, but for now, the U.S.-ROK Combined Forces Command stands ready to repel aggression. Allied soldiers, to include a few U.S. infantrymen, still patrol the Demilitarized Zone, man the barrier fences, and wait to provide quick-reaction forces, dutifully working within the system devised by the UNC over twenty years ago. South Korean ships, planes, and coast watchers observe the sea approaches, enforcing schemes evolved by General Bonesteel's headquarters. Behind the borders, ROK soldiers, police, and

| | |
|---|---|
| 20 November 1974 | A combined U.S.-ROK investigation team tripped a KPA booby trap while examining a KPA tunnel complex, 1 U.S. KIA, 6 U.S. WIA. |
| 18 August 1976 | KPA guards in the Joint Security Area attacked a U.S.-ROK tree-cutting party, 2 U.S. KIA, 4 U.S. WIA. |
| 14 July 1977 | DPRK forces shot down a U.S. CH-47 helicopter that strayed north of the DMZ, 3 U.S. KIA, 1 U.S. briefly held prisoner. |
| 6 December 1979 | A U.S. 2d Infantry Division patrol (1-9 Infantry) became lost and tripped a mine on the KPA side of the DMZ, 1 U.S. KIA, 4 U.S. WIA, and unknown KPA losses. |
| 28 August 1982 | A U.S. 2d Infantry Division soldier (1-31 Infantry) defected to the DPRK |

Source: Finley, *The US Military Experience in Korea*, 178—241.

Figure 12. DMZ incidents involving casualties to U.S. forces (since 3 December 1969)

militia guard the interior, carrying out programs begun under President Park in 1967—68.

To date, this massive security effort has been sufficient. Neither the Americans nor the South Koreans have lapsed into the sort of complacency that prevailed in the early 1960s. Instead, it appears that the allies have kept in mind the prescient words of General Maxwell Taylor as he announced the armistice of 27 July 1953: "There is no occasion for celebration or boisterous conduct. We are faced with the same enemy, only a short distance away, and must be ready for any moves he makes."[26] Bolstered by the lessons learned in the Second Korean Conflict, the vigil continues.

# Appendix 1

## The Second Korean Conflict— A Chronology of Key Events

**1966**

1 Sep    General Charles H. Bonesteel III, USA, assumed duties as Commander in Chief, United Nations Command; Commander, U.S. Forces, Korea; and Commanding General, U.S. Eighth Army.

5 Oct    Kim Il-sung addressed the Second Korean Workers' Party Conference. He vowed immediate, vigorous efforts to subvert the ROK and fight the United States. He also installed a cadre of hard-liners to prosecute his new insurgency policies.

31 Oct   U.S. President Lyndon B. Johnson arrived in Seoul for a state visit.

2 Nov    U.S. patrol ambushed with six killed. This signaled the start of the Second Korean Conflict.

6 Nov    Commander, U.S. Eighth Army, formed his Special Working Group to address the changed threat from the DPRK.

**1967**

9 Feb    Special Working Group recommendations implemented. This comprised the rudiments of the UNC campaign plan to meet the new northern challenge.

12 Apr   ROK troops employed artillery to repulse a company of KPA soldiers. This was the first U.S.-ROK use of artillery since the armistice. It reflected new, more discretionary Eighth Army rules of engagement.

22 May   A bomb planted by North Korean terrorists destroyed a U.S. barracks well south of the DMZ.

1 Jun    Ambassador William J. Porter replaced Ambassador Winthrop G. Brown as U.S. representative in Seoul.

| | |
|---|---|
| 28 Jul | New barrier test fence construction began in U.S. sector of DMZ. |
| 28 Sep | U.S. troops completed the anti-infiltration fence in their sector. One battalion of U.S. 7th Infantry Division joined the U.S. 2d Infantry Division to start a new rotation system that placed four maneuver battalions on the DMZ and a fifth in reserve as a quick-reaction force. |
| 3 Oct | Commanding General, U.S. Eighth Army, released his proposed Counterinfiltration-Guerrilla Concepts Requirements Plan, his resource forecast for the Second Korean Conflict. |
| 15 Dec | ROK Presidential Instruction #18 issued. It delineated new ROK counterinsurgency goals and actions. |

**1968**

| | |
|---|---|
| 17 Jan | A platoon from the KPA's elite 124th Army Unit infiltrated through the U.S. sector of the DMZ. They intended to assassinate ROK President Park Chung Hee. |
| 20 Jan | Raid on the Blue House detected and repulsed. ROK losses totaled sixty-eight killed and sixty-six wounded. |
| 23 Jan | USS *Pueblo* (AGER-2) was seized by KPN patrol boats—one killed, eighty-two captured U.S. men. United States implemented an air and sea buildup in and around the ROK. President Johnson activated 14,787 reservists to support the show of force. |
| 31 Jan | Tet Offensive started in Vietnam. |
| 11 Feb | U.S. envoy Cyrus Vance arrived to discuss U.S.-ROK approaches to the deepening Korean crisis. |
| 15 Feb | ROK President Park Chung Hee ordered creation of a popular militia, the Homeland Defense Reserve Force. This was formally announced in mid-April. Additional measures strengthened the ROK intelligence agencies, police, and military for counterguerrilla work. |
| 21 Mar | A brigade headquarters of the U.S. 7th Infantry Division deployed north to assist in command of U.S. forces along the DMZ. |
| 1 Apr | Combat pay authorized for U.S. troops north of the Imjin River. |
| 17 Apr | President Park and President Johnson met in Honolulu to coordinate allied strategy. |
| 1 Jun | U.S. Congress approved an emergency $100 million Military Assistance Program grant for the ROK. |
| 30 Jul | ROK First Army completed its portion of the DMZ anti-infiltration fence. Linked into the U.S. fence that had been built in 1967, the new barrier ran along the entire length of the DMZ. |

| | |
|---|---|
| 21 Aug | DPRK agents' boat intercepted and sunk in combined effort between ROKN, ROKAF, USAF, and ROK CIA. |
| 30 Aug | First two of twenty planned ROK "Reconstruction Villages" opened just south of the DMZ. Discharged ROK Army veterans and their families lived in these villages. |
| 24 Sep | ROK Army units battled a small battalion of KPA troops south of the DMZ. |
| 15 Oct | The ROK-U.S. Operational Planning Staff formed to coordinate ROK defense. Until now, ROK officers had no official voice in United Nations Command planning. |
| 30 Oct | Ulchin-Samchok landing began. KPA 124th Army Unit troops attempted to foment a guerrilla movement. KPA force eliminated. ROK losses totaled sixty-three dead and fifty-five wounded. |
| 23 Dec | USS *Pueblo* crew released from captivity. |

## 1969

| | |
|---|---|
| 1 Jan | In a major shake-up, Kim Il-sung removed and denounced key leaders in his anti-ROK operations. |
| 7 Mar | ROK Army formed two antiguerrilla brigades from their special forces elements. |
| 17 Mar | Exercise Focus Retina demonstrated U.S. ability to reinforce the U.S. Eighth Army; a U.S. airborne brigade flew in from the continental United States. |
| 15 Apr | KPAF fighters shot down a U.S. Navy EC-121M aircraft over the Sea of Japan. Thirty-one Americans died. A U.S. naval show of force followed. |
| 5 Jun | The last American reservists departed Korea. They had been called up in response to the USS *Pueblo* incident. |
| 26 Jul | U.S. President Richard M. Nixon announced what became known as the "Guam Doctrine" or "Nixon Doctrine." In short, he promised American advice and equipment for allies but warned them not to expect commitments of ground troops. U.S. overseas troop contingents, including those in Korea, would be reduced in size. |
| 25 Aug | President Park met with President Nixon in San Francisco to discuss implementation of the Guam Doctrine in the Korean theater. |
| 29 Aug | The first six American-made F-4D Phantom II fighter jets were turned over to the ROKAF. |
| 1 Oct | General John H. Michaelis succeeded General Bonesteel as Commander in Chief, United Nations Command; Com- |

|         | mander, U.S. Forces, Korea; and Commanding General, U.S. Eighth Army. |
|---------|---|
| 18 Oct  | A U.S. jeep was ambushed with four killed. These were the last U.S. casualties in the Second Korean Conflict. |
| 3 Dec   | The DPRK returned three captured American helicopter crewmen. |

# Appendix 2

## U.S. Forces, Korea, Order of Battle, 1 January 1968

*Combined and Joint Headquarters*
    U.S. Eighth Army-U.S. Forces, Korea-UN Command—Yongsan
        Military Armistice Commission (MAC) Delegation—Panmunjom
        Korean Military Assistance Group (KMAG)—Yongsan

*U.S. Army* (about 50,000 soldiers)
    U.S. Army Support Group, Joint Security Area—Panmunjom
    U.S. Army Advisory Group, Korea—Yongsan
        2d Engineer Group (construction)—Yongsan
        4th Missile Command (supporting ROK First Army)—Chunchon
    Eighth Army Depot Command-Eighth Army Rear—Taegu
    Eighth Army Special Troops—Yongsan
    Eighth Army Support Command—Yongsan
    38th Artillery Brigade (Air Defense)—Osan AB
    I Corps (Group)
        2d Infantry Division(+)—Camp Howze
        7th Infantry Division(-)—Camp Casey
        I Corps (Group) Artillery—Camp St. Barbara

*U.S. Air Force* (about 5,000 airmen)
    U.S. Air Forces Korea—Osan AB
    6145th Air Force Advisory Group—Osan AB
    314th Air Division—Osan, Kimpo, Kunsan ABs
        3d Tactical Fighter Wing—Kunsan AB
    611th Military Airlift Command Support Squadron—Kimpo AB
    6314th Support Wing—Osan AB

*U.S. Navy-U.S. Marine Corps* (about 500 sailors and Marines)
    U.S. Naval Forces Korea—Chinhae, Pohang
    U.S. Naval Advisory Group—Chinhae

Sources: General Charles H. Bonesteel III, USA, "On Korea's DMZ: Vigil Seals the 'Porous' War," *Army* (November 1968):58—6C; "Pacific Air Forces," *Air Force and Space Digest* (September 1968): 83—84.

# Appendix 3, Annex 1

## Tactical Disposition of Korean People's Army Maneuver Forces, 1 January 1968

### Along the DMZ (West to East)

2d Army Group
    2d Corps
        6th Infantry Division
        8th Infantry Division
        9th Infantry Division (in depth, corps reserve)

    7th Corps
        15th Infantry Division
        45th Infantry Division
        5th Infantry Division (in depth, corps reserve)

    2d Army Group reserves
        3d Motorized Infantry Division
        101st Medium Tank Regiment

1st Army Group
    5th Corps
        4th Infantry Division (in depth, corps reserve)
        12th Infantry Division
        46th Infantry Division
        25th Infantry Brigade

    4th Corps
        2d Infantry Division (in depth, corps reserve)
        13th Infantry Division
        47th Infantry Division
        111th Independent Infantry Regiment

    1st Army Group reserve
        103d Medium Tank Regiment

### In the Northern Democratic People's Republic of Korea

    1st Corps
        7th Infantry Division

      10th Infantry Division
      104th Medium Tank Regiment

3d Corps
      1st Motorized Infantry Division
      37th Infantry Division
      102d Medium Tank Regiment

6th Corps
      26th Infantry Brigade
      27th Motorized Infantry Division
      28th Infantry Division

National Reserves
      20th Infantry Brigade
      22d Infantry Brigade
      24th Infantry Brigade
      105th Tank Division
      106th Heavy Tank Regiment

Ten cadre-strength reserve divisions
      (Cadre unit designations unknown. These reserve component formations were probably located in the interior of the DPRK, although some may have supplemented coastal-defense border guards.)

Sources: Joseph G. Bermudez, *North Korean Special Forces* (London: Jane's Publishing Co., Ltd., 1988), 5—6, 154—55, 160—62, 169—73; Suck-ho Lee, "Party-Military Relations in North Korea: A Comparative Analysis" (Ph.D. dissertation, George Washington University, 1983), 154, 219; Emerson Chapin, "Success Story in South Korea," *Foreign Affairs* (April 1969):565; Sung An Tai, *North Korea in Transition* (Westport, CT: Greenwood Press, 1983), 16—18; Frederica Bunge, ed., *North Korea: A Country Study* (Washington, DC: U.S. Government Printing Office, 1981), 229—31.

# Appendix 3, Annex 2

## Tactical Disposition of U.S. Eighth Army Maneuver Forces, 1 January 1968

*Frontline Units on and Near the DMZ (West to East)*

    Defending Seoul: I Corps (Group)
        ROK 5th Marine Brigade
        ROK 98th Regimental Combat Team[1]
        U.S. 2d Infantry Division(+)
        ROK VI Corps
            ROK 25th Infantry Division
            ROK 28th Infantry Division
            ROK 20th Infantry Division
        Forces in depth: ROK I Corps (Group)
            U.S. 7th Infantry Division(-)[2]

    Central and Eastern Republic of Korea: ROK First Army[3]
        ROK 6th Infantry Division
        ROK 3d Infantry Division
        ROK 15th Infantry Division
        ROK 7th Infantry Division
        ROK 21st Infantry Division
        ROK 12th Infantry Division
        Forces in depth: ROK First Army
            ROK 1st Armored Brigade
            ROK 2d Armored Brigade
            ROK 2d Infantry Division
            ROK 5th Infantry Division
            ROK 8th Infantry Division
            ROK 11th Infantry Division
            ROK 26th Infantry Division
            ROK 27th Infantry Division
            ROK 29th Infantry Division
            ROK 32d Ready Reserve Infantry Division(-)[4]

*Units in the Southern Republic of Korea: ROK Second Army*

ROK Marine Division(-)

ROK Reserve Components
    ROK 30th Ready Reserve Infantry Division
    ROK 33d Ready Reserve Infantry Division
    ROK 38th Ready Reserve Infantry Division
    ROK 51st Ready Reserve Infantry Division
    ROK 31st Rear Area Security Division
    ROK 35th Rear Area Security Division
    ROK 36th Rear Area Security Division
    ROK 37th Rear Area Security Division
    ROK 39th Rear Area Security Division
    ROK 50th Rear Area Security Division

*Deployed to the Republic of Vietnam:*

ROK Forces Vietnam Field Command
    ROK Capital Division
    ROK 9th Infantry Division
    ROK 2d Marine Brigade

[1]From the ROK 32d Ready Reserve Infantry Division, under operational control of the U.S. 2d Infantry Division.

[2]Includes the 22d Royal Thai Company.

[3]ROK units organized into corps for combat. There are no reliable unclassified listings that depict the exact composition of these corps, other than ROK VI Corps in the U.S. sector.

[4]The ROK 32d Ready Reserve Infantry Division went on active duty to help fill the gap created by the departure of forces to Vietnam. It was replaced in ROK Second Army by the newly organized ROK 51st Ready Reserve Infantry.

Sources: Shelby L. Stanton, *Vietnam Order of Battle* (Washington, DC: U.S. News Books, 1981), 272—73; General Charles H. Bonesteel III, USA, "General Bonesteel's Year End Press Conference, 11 January 1967," transcript from personal papers of Colonel Walter B. Clark, USA (ret.), Charleston, SC.

# Appendix 4

## Significant U.S.-KPA Firefights, November 1966—December 1969

| | |
|---|---|
| 2 Nov 66 | U.S. 2d Infantry Division patrol (1-23 Infantry) ambushed south of DMZ. Six U.S. KIA, one KATUSA KIA, one U.S. WIA; unknown KPA losses. |
| 12 Feb 67 | U.S. 2d Infantry Division patrol (3-23 Infantry) ambushed south of DMZ. One U.S. KIA; unknown KPA losses. |
| 5 Apr 67 | U.S. 2d Infantry Division guard post engaged KPA infiltrators south of DMZ. No U.S. losses; five KPA KIA. |
| 29 Apr 67 | U.S. 2d Infantry Division patrol ambushed KPA infiltrators south of DMZ. No U.S. losses; one KPA KIA, one KPA WIA, one KPA captured. |
| 22 May 67 | U.S. 2d Infantry Division barracks (1-23 Infantry) demolished by daylight explosion south of DMZ. Two U.S. KIA, seventeen U.S. WIA; no KPA losses. |
| 16 Jul 67 | U.S. 2d Infantry Division guard post attacked south of DMZ. Three U.S. KIA, two U.S. WIA; unknown KPA losses. |
| 10 Aug 67 | U.S. 7th Infantry Division construction team (13th Engineers) ambushed well south of DMZ in daylight. Three U.S. KIA, sixteen U.S. WIA; unknown KPA losses. |
| 22 Aug 67 | U.S. 2d Infantry Division jeep destroyed by mine and ambush south of DMZ. One U.S. KIA, one U.S. WIA; unknown KPA losses. |
| 28 Aug 67 | U.S. Eighth Army construction team (76th Engineers) ambushed in daylight near the Joint Security Area but still south of the DMZ. Two U.S. KIA, two KATUSA KIA, fourteen U.S. WIA, nine KATUSA WIA, three civilians WIA; unknown KPA losses. |
| 29 Aug 67 | U.S. 2d Infantry Division jeep destroyed by mine south of DMZ. Three U.S. KIA, five U.S. WIA; no KPA losses. |

| | |
|---|---|
| 7 Oct 67 | U.S. 2d Infantry Division patrol boat ambushed on Imjin River south of DMZ. One U.S. KIA; unknown KPA losses. |
| 22 Jan 68 | U.S. 2d Infantry Division guard post engaged by KPA infiltrators. Three U.S. WIA; unknown KPA losses. |
| 24 Jan 68 | U.S. 2d Infantry Division defensive position (1-23 Infantry) attacked south of DMZ by KPA 124th Army Unit exfiltrators. Two U.S. KIA; three KPA WIA. |
| 26 Jan 68 | U.S. 2d Infantry Division defensive position (2-72 Armor) attacked south of DMZ by KPA 124th Army Unit exfiltrators. One U.S. KIA; unknown KPA losses. |
| 29 Jan 68 | U.S. 2d Infantry Division patrols and outposts engaged and repulsed four teams of KPA infiltrators. No U.S. losses; unknown KPA losses. |
| 6 Feb 68 | U.S. 2d Infantry Division guard post attacked. No U.S. losses; one KPA WIA. |
| 27 Mar 68 | U.S. 2d Infantry Division reaction forces and ROK 25th Infantry Division ambushed KPA infiltrators. No U.S. losses; three KPA KIA. |
| 14 Apr 68 | U.S. Army Support Group truck ambushed south of the Joint Security Area in daylight. Two U.S. KIA, two KATUSA KIA, two U.S. WIA; unknown KPA losses. |
| 21 Apr 68 | U.S. 7th Infantry Division patrol (2-31 Infantry) engaged KPA infiltrator company in the DMZ. One U.S. KIA, three U.S. WIA; five KPA KIA, fifteen KPA WIA. |
| 27 Apr 68 | U.S. 7th Infantry Division patrol (2-31 Infantry) ambushed in the DMZ. One KATUSA KIA, two U.S. WIA; unknown KPA losses. |
| 3 Jul 68 | U.S. 2d Infantry Division patrol ambushed in the DMZ. One U.S. WIA; unknown KPA losses. |
| 20 Jul 68 | U.S. 2d Infantry Division patrol ambushed in the DMZ. One U.S. KIA; unknown KPA losses. U.S. 7th Infantry Division patrol (1-32 Infantry) ambushed in the DMZ. One U.S. KIA; unknown KPA losses. |
| 21 Jul 68 | U.S. 2d Infantry Division patrol (2-38 Infantry) ambushed in the DMZ. One U.S. WIA, one KATUSA WIA. |
| 30 Jul 68 | U.S. 2d Infantry Division patrol (3-23 Infantry) ambushed in the DMZ. One U.S. KIA, three U.S. WIA; unknown KPA losses. |
| 5 Aug 68 | U.S. 2d Infantry Division patrol (1-38 Infantry) ambushed south of the DMZ in daylight. One U.S. KIA, four U.S. WIA; one KPA KIA. |

| | |
|---|---|
| 18 Aug 68 | U.S. 7th Infantry Division patrol (1-32 Infantry) ambushed south of the DMZ. Two U.S. KIA; two KPA WIA. |
| 19 Sep 68 | U.S. 2d Infantry Division patrols (2-38 Infantry) and quick-reaction forces (4-7 Cavalry, 2-9 Infantry [Mechanized], 2d Division Counter Agent Company) isolated and destroyed KPA infiltrator squad. Two KATUSA KIA, six KATUSA WIA; four KPA KIA, one KPA WIA. |
| 27 Sep 68 | U.S. 2d Infantry Division jeep ambushed in the DMZ. Two U.S. KIA; unknown KPA losses. |
| 3 Oct 68 | U.S. 7th Infantry Division guard post (1-31 Infantry) engaged KPA exfiltrator south of DMZ. No U.S. losses; one KPA KIA. |
| 5 Oct 68 | U.S. 2d Infantry Division patrol ambushed in the DMZ. One U.S. KIA, two U.S. WIA; unknown KPA losses. |
| 10 Oct 68 | U.S. 2d Infantry Division boat patrol engaged KPA infiltrator crossing the Imjin River. No U.S. losses; one KPA KIA. |
| 11 Oct 68 | U.S. 2d Infantry Division ambushed KPA infiltrators in the DMZ. No U.S. losses; two KPA KIA. |
| 23 Oct 68 | U.S. 2d Infantry Division patrol engaged KPA infiltrators in the DMZ. One U.S. KIA, five U.S. WIA; one KPA KIA. |
| 23 Jan 69 | U.S. 2d Infantry Division guard posts repulsed KPA infiltrators. No U.S. losses; unknown KPA losses. |
| 4 Feb 69 | U.S. 2d Infantry Division guard posts repulsed KPA infiltrators. No U.S. losses; unknown KPA losses. |
| 13 Mar 69 | U.S. 2d Infantry Division fence repair patrol (2-38 Infantry) engaged by KPA infiltrators. No U.S. losses; unknown KPA losses. |
| 15 Mar 69 | U.S. 2d Infantry Division marker maintenance patrol ambushed in the DMZ. One U.S. KIA, two U.S. WIA, one KATUSA WIA. Medical evacuation helicopter crashed after takeoff, killing five fliers and the three wounded. |
| 16 Mar 69 | U.S. 2d Infantry Division patrol engaged KPA infiltrators in the DMZ. No U.S. losses; unknown KPA losses. |
| 20 Mar 69 | U.S. 2d Infantry Division patrol engaged KPA patrol in the DMZ. No U.S. losses; unknown KPA losses. |
| 29 Mar 69 | U.S. 2d Infantry Division patrol engaged KPA patrol in the DMZ. No U.S. losses; unknown KPA losses. |
| 15 May 69 | U.S. 2d Infantry Division patrol engaged KPA infiltrator. One U.S. WIA, one KATUSA WIA; unknown KPA losses. |

| | |
|---|---|
| 20 May 69 | U.S. 2d Infantry Division guard post engaged KPA infiltrators. No U.S. losses; one KPA KIA. |
| 21 Jul 69 | U.S. 2d Infantry Division guard posts engaged and repulsed KPA infiltrators. No U.S. losses; unknown KPA losses. |
| 17 Aug 69 | U.S. Eighth Army helicopter (59th Aviation Company) strayed north of the DMZ and was shot down. Three U.S. captured. |
| 18 Oct 69 | U.S. 7th Infantry Division jeep ambushed in the DMZ. Four U.S. KIA; unknown KPA losses. |

Sources: James P. Finley, *The US Military Experience in Korea, 1871—1982* (Yongsan, Korea: Command Historian, USFK/EUSA, 1983), 116—35; Headquarters, 3d Brigade, 2d Infantry Division, "Annual Historical Supplement 1966," "Annual Historical Supplement 1967," "Annual Historical Supplement 1968," "Annual Historical Supplement 1969," and Headquarters, 2d Brigade, 2d Infantry Division, "Annual Historical Supplement 1968," Military History Institute Archives, Carlisle Barracks, PA.

# Notes

## Introduction

The epigraph comes from General of the Army Omar N. Bradley's testimony to Congress in the wake of General of the Army Douglas MacArthur's relief from command in Korea. Bradley believed that the primary U.S. concern was not the Chinese enemy in Korea but the Soviet threat to exhausted, war-weary Western Europe. See Omar Nelson Bradley and Clay Blair, *A General's Life* (New York: Simon and Schuster, 1983), 558.

1. Andrew F. Krepinevich, Jr., *The Army and Vietnam* (Baltimore, MD: Johns Hopkins University Press, 1986), 37.

2. Phillip B. Davidson, *Vietnam at War, 1946—1975: The History* (Novato, CA: Presidio Press, 1988), 730.

3. United States Department of the Army, FM 100-20, *Military Operations in Low-Intensity Conflict (Final Draft)* (Washington, DC, 7 March 1989), 1—1 to 1—12.

## Chapter 1

The epigraph is from Sun-tzu, *The Art of War*, translated and with an introduction by Samuel B. Griffith (New York: Oxford University Press, 1971), 63.

1. United States, Congress, Senate, Committee on Foreign Relations, *The United States and the Korean Problem: Documents, 1943—1953*, 83d Cong., 1st Sess. (Washington, DC, 1953), Document 74, Preamble to the Korean Armistice Agreement. This publication is cited hereafter as Senate, *The United States and the Korean Problem*.

2. Frederica M. Bunge, ed., *South Korea: A Country Study*, Area handbook series (Washington, DC: United States Department of the Army, 1981), 43, 202.

3. Ibid., 27; Joungwon A. Kim, "North Korea's New Offensive," *Foreign Affairs* 48 (October 1969):174—75; and Suck-ho Lee, "Party-Military Relations in North Korea: A Comparative Analysis," Ph.D. dissertation, George Washington University, 1983, 153, 166—67. Lee, a 1968 graduate of the Korean Military Academy, participated in the Second Korean Conflict.

4. Bunge, *South Korea*, 29—34, 39; and Se-jin Kim, *The Politics of Military Revolution in Korea* (Chapel Hill: University of North Carolina Press, 1971), 89—91. Park, born in the countryside, had been commissioned through an officer candidate school in 1946. He had risen mainly through staff and intelligence work, although he did have the opportunity to attend the U.S. Army Field Artillery Officer Advanced Course at Fort Sill, Oklahoma.

5. Lee, "Party-Military Relations," 153—56, 189—93.

6. Ibid., 153, 175, 182, 189—93; Tai Sung An, *North Korea in Transition: From Dictatorship to Dynasty* (Westport, CT: Greenwood Press, 1983), 16—18; and Joseph S. Bermudez, Jr., *North Korean Special Forces* (Surrey, England: Jane's Publishing Co., 1988), 28—29.

7. "Party-Military Relations," 153.

8. Lyndon B. Johnson, *The Vantage Point: Perspectives of the Presidency, 1963—1969* (New York: Holt, Rinehart, and Winston, 1971), 358; and James P. Finley, *The US Military Experience in Korea, 1971—1982: In the Vanguard of ROK-US Relations* (San Francisco, CA: Command Historian's Office, Secretary Joint Staff, HQ, USFK/EUSA, 1983), 114—15.

9. Finley, *US Military Experience in Korea*, 114—15.

10. Lee, "Party-Military Relations," 153—54.

11. Finley, *US Military Experience in Korea*, 31, 127—27.

12. Jeffrey Simon, "NATO and Warsaw Pact Institutional Developments," in his *NATO Warsaw Pact Force Mobilization* (Washington, DC: National Defense University Press, 1988), 41—42; and William C. Westmoreland, *A Soldier Reports* (New York: Doubleday and Co., 1976), 499, 505; and Harry G. Summers, *On Strategy: The Vietnam War in Context* (Carlisle Barracks, PA: United States Army War College, April 1981), 91.

13. Finley, *US Military Experience in Korea*, 31, 127.

14. United States, Armed Forces Staff College, AFSC Pub 1, *The Joint Staff Officer's Guide* (Washington, DC: United States Government Printing Office, 1988), 45.

15. Ibid., 49.

16. West Point Alumni Foundation, *Register of Graduates and Former Cadets, 1969* (West Point, NY, 1969), 183, 314, 418; General Charles H. Bonesteel III, "U.S.-South Korean Partnership Holds a Truculent North at Bay," *Army* 19 (October 1969):60; and David Halberstam, *The Best and the Brightest* (New York: Fawcett Crest, 1971), 890.

17. Colonel Walter B. Clark, United States Army (ret.), telephone conversation with author from Charleston, South Carolina, 25 March 1990. Colonel Clark was the senior aide-de-camp and executive officer to General Charles H. Bonesteel III from September 1966 until August 1967.

18. Trevor Armbrister, *A Matter of Accountability: The True Story of the Pueblo Affair* (New York: Coward McCann, 1970), 119.

19. Clark interview; and General Charles H. Bonesteel III, United States Army (ret.), interview with Lieutenant Colonel Robert St. Louis, p. 328, Senior Officers Oral History Program Project 73—2, 1973, United States Army Military History Institute, Carlisle Barracks, PA. The institute is cited hereafter as USAMHI.

20. Bonesteel interview, 334—35.

21. Ibid., 335—36.

22. Clark interview.

23. Bonesteel interview, 328; and Finley, *US Military Experience in Korea*, 220.

24. Bonesteel interview, 334.

25. United States, Department of the Army, FM 100-5, *Operations* (Washington, DC: United States Government Printing Office, 19 February 1962), 47.

26. Lee, "Party-Military Relations," 169—79; and United States, Department of State, "Background Notes: North Korea" (Washington, DC: United States Government Printing Office, September 1968), 3.

27. Lee, "Party-Military Relations," 210—16; L. James Binder, "On the Line in Korea: The Porous War," *Army* 19 (January 1969):57; and United States, Congress, Senate, Committee on Armed Services, *Combat Readiness of United States and South Korean Forces in South Korea*, 90th Cong., 2d Sess. (Washington, DC, 7 June 1968), 2—3. See appendix 3, annex 1, of this study for more details on the North Korean order of battle and probable deployment. This Senate publication is cited hereafter as Senate, *Combat Readiness*.

28. Binder, "The Porous War," 57; Institute for Strategic Studies, *The Military Balance, 1968—69* (London: Adlard and Son, 1968), 13; and Lieutenant Colonel Everett H. Webster, United States Air Force, "Is the Morning Calm About to Be Broken in Korea?" Research

report no. 4471, Air War College, Air University, Maxwell Air Force Base, AL, March 1971, 13—14, 18.

29. Senate, *Combat Readiness*, 3; and Institute for Strategic Studies, *The Military Balance, 1968—69*, 13.

30. Senate, *Combat Readiness*, 3.

31. Webster, "Morning Calm," 14.

32. Senate, *Combat Readiness*, 3.

33. Bermudez, *North Korean Special Forces*, 26—31, 86.

34. Bonesteel interview, 329—31; and Bermudez, *North Korean Special Forces*, 31, 86—87, 103.

35. Binder, "The Porous War," 57; and Bermudez, *North Korean Special Forces*, 8.

36. Colonel William P. Guthrie, United States Army, "Korea: The Other DMZ," *Infantry* 60 (March-April 1970):17.

37. Bunge, *South Korea*, 52—54.

38. Bermudez, *North Korean Special Forces*, 169—70.

39. Senate, *The United States and the Korean Problem*, Document 74, Articles 1—11, 23, 27, Korean Armistice Agreement.

40. Bermudez, *North Korean Special Forces*, 87; and Bunge, *South Korea*, 58.

41. Bunge, *South Korea*, 49.

42. Ibid, 54, 61, 77, 86.

43. Emerson Chapin, "Success Story in South Korea," *Foreign Affairs* 47 (April 1969):561.

44. See appendix 3, annex 2, of this study for more details on the U.S.-ROK order of battle and likely deployment.

45. Major Vandon E. Jenerette, United States Army, "The Forgotten DMZ," *Military Review* 68 (May 1988):40.

46. Bonesteel interview, 332; and Captain Rush R. Wicker, United States Army, "CH-37 Mojave—Workhorse of Korea," *United States Army Aviation Digest* 14 (July 1968):32—34.

47. Shelby L. Stanton, *Vietnam Order of Battle* (Washington, DC: U.S. News Books, 1981), 287; and United States Army, 2d Infantry Division, "Operational Report—Lessons Learned, Headquarters, 2d Infantry Division, Period Ending 30 April 1969 (U)," 10, Archives, Combined Arms Research Library, United States Army Command and General Staff College, Fort Leavenworth, KS, hereafter cited as 2ID, "Operational Report . . . 30 April 1969." The library is cited hereafter as CARL.

48. Clark Dougan, et al., eds., *A Nation Divided, The Vietnam Experience*, vol. 20 (Boston, MA: Boston Publishing Co., 1984), 78, 80.

49. Senate, *Combat Readiness*, 4; Finley, *US Military Experience in Korea*, 60; and Colonel Charles L. Bachtel, United States Army (ret.), "The KATUSA Program," *Signal* 23 (December 1968): 42—44.

50. Guthrie, "Korea: The Other DMZ," 20.

51. Binder, "The Porous War," 57.

52. Guthrie, "Korea: The Other DMZ," 22; and Clark interview.

53. Wesley Pruden, Jr., "Asia's Other War," *Army* 17 (November 1967):31.

54. Binder, "The Porous War," 57.

55. Senate, *Combat Readiness*, 9; and Bunge, *South Korea*, 231—32.

56. Paul S. Crane, M.D., "Korean Attitudes and Thought Patterns—Prepared for UNC/USFK," in the personal papers of Colonel Walter B. Clark, United States Army (ret.), Charleston,

SC; Bonesteel interview, 329, 338; and Clark interview. See also General Westmoreland's similar observations in *A Soldier Reports*, 313—14.

57. Webster, "Morning Calm," 18.
58. Finley, *US Military Experience in Korea*, 20; and Senate, *Combat Readiness*, 9.
59. Bermudez, *North Korean Special Forces*, 23—24; Bunge, *South Korea*, 240—42; and Larry Cable, *A Conflict of Myths: The Development of American Counterinsurgency Doctrine and the Vietnam War* (New York: New York University Press, 1986), 33—43.
60. Finley, *US Military Experience in Korea*, 105.

## Chapter 2

The epigraph comes from Wesley Pruden, Jr., "Asia's Other War," 28.

1. Finley, *US Military Experience in Korea*, 114—15, 220; and Bonesteel interview, 329.
2. Lee, "Party-Military Relations," 151—54.
3. Kim Il-song, "The International Situation and Problems of the World Communist Movement," in his *Revolution and Socialist Construction in Korea: Selected Writings* (New York: International Publishers, 1971), 114—15; and Bermudez, *North Korean Special Forces*, 30.
4. Lee, "Party-Military Relations," 153—54; and U.S. Department of State, "Background Notes: North Korea," 3.
5. An, *North Korea*, 16—18; Bermudez, *North Korean Special Forces*, 31; and Bonesteel interview, 328.
6. Kim Il-song, "The International Situation," 113.
7. Finley, *US Military Experience in Korea*, 116.
8. Ibid., 116; and Clark interview. President Johnson visited Vietnam, the Philippines, Thailand, and Malaysia before landing in Korea.
9. Jenerette, "The Forgotten DMZ," 35—36; Pruden, "Asia's Other War," 28; United States Army, 2d Infantry Division, 3d Brigade, "Annual Historical Supplement 1966," USAMHI; Clark interview; "DOD Order Curbs 'Premature' Medal of Honor Information," *Army Times*, 16 November 1966:5. Those who believe in the whims of fortune might observe that the ambushed patrol's chain of command included descendants of two of the American military's more unlucky generals. Major General George Pickett (U.S. 2d Infantry Division) was a cousin of the unfortunate Confederate who led the doomed charge at Gettysburg. Colonel Alan W. Jones, Jr. (3d Brigade) had been captured in the Battle of the Bulge when German forces surrounded the bulk of his father's ill-starred 106th Infantry Division. In Pickett's case, the general compounded his misfortune by insisting that his lost patrol had fought superbly. He even publicly recommended the award of a Medal of Honor to one of his dead soldiers. Secretary of Defense Robert S. McNamara censured Pickett for this improper outburst.
10. Jenerette, "The Forgotten DMZ," 35—36; and Johnson, *The Vantage Point*, 363. Though Johnson referred to his trip to Korea, he made no mention of the patrol casualties in his memoirs.
11. Bonesteel interview, 328.
12. Westmoreland, *A Soldier Reports*, 90; and Stuart L. Perkins, "The US Force Structure and C3," in *Guerrilla Warfare and Counterinsurgency: U.S.-Soviet Policy in the Third World*, edited by Richard H. Schultz, Jr., et al. (Lexington, MA: Lexington Books, 1989), 242—43.
13. Bonesteel interview, 328.
14. General Charles H. Bonesteel III, United States Army (ret.), "On Korea's DMZ: Vigil

Seals the 'Porous' War," *Army* 18 (October 1968):60; Senate, *Combat Readiness*, 3; and Bonesteel interview, 329—30.

15. Bonesteel interview, 329.

16. United States, Department of the Army, FM 100-15, *Field Service Regulations: Larger Units*, With Change 1 (Washington DC: United States Government Printing Office, 16 March 1966), 3. The contemporary core doctrinal manual from which FM 100-5 derived was the 1962 version of FM 100-5, *Field Service Regulations: Operations*. It featured a slightly better theoretical discussion of the various types of warfare, although admitting that "the dividing line between cold war and limited war is neither distinct nor absolute." FM 100-5 (1962), 5. Like FM 100-15, FM 100-5 then proceeds to list "local aggression," "conventional war," and "limited nuclear war" as examples of limited war, tying the whole sloppy bundle together by saying that "a limited war is any conflict which does not involve the unrestricted employment of all available resources." Ibid., 5. Finally, just to muddy things up, FM 100-5 differs from FM 100-15 by indicating that cold war situations "can and often do" involve overt combat. Ibid., 155.

 Most of the ideas, good and bad, in the other manuals discussed in this study can be traced back to phrases, sentences, and paragraphs in FM 100-5. See Krepinevich, *The Army and Vietnam*, 39, for critical analysis of this manual.

17. FM 100-20, 1—10 to 1—12. Curiously, one part of FM 100-5 (1962) that did not find its way into other manuals was a brief discussion of situations "short of war," listed as including "show of force, truce enforcement, international police action," and "legal occupation." FM 100-5 (1962), 156. Unfortunately, there was no specific definition or discussion of these operations. Instead, the authors supplied very general (and somewhat useful) guidance for all situations of this type. This general guidance did percolate down to the segment on "Cold War" missions in the divisional manual.

18. FM 100-15, 35—37.

19. United States, Department of the Army, FM 61-100, *The Division* (Washington, DC: United States Government Printing Office, June 1965), 146—49. This lifts whole chunks from FM 100-5 (1962), 160—61.

20. United States, Department of the Army, FM 31-16, *Counterguerrilla Operations* (Washington, DC: United States Government Printing Office, 19 February 1963), 71—74; and Krepinevich, *The Army and Vietnam*, 39—41, 127.

21. United States, Department of the Army, FM 61-100, *The Division* (Washington, DC: United States Government Printing Office, November 1968), 12—15 to 12—18. Indicative of the lack of doctrinal development during the Vietnam era, this manual repeats almost verbatim the entire "Cold War" segment referenced in note 19 above. The only notable change, aside from some adjustments for grammatical clarity, is the substitution of the term "stability operations" for "counterinsurgency."

22. Krepinevich, *The Army and Vietnam*, 197, features the terse Westmoreland quote concerning fire power as the answer to counterinsurgency. See also Robert A. Doughty, *The Evolution of US Army Tactical Doctrine, 1946—76*, Leavenworth Papers no. 1 (Fort Leavenworth, KS: Combat Studies Institute, United States Army Command and General Staff College, August 1979), 39.

23. Bonesteel interview, 335.

24. Ibid. The innovations developed in Korea during the late 1960s were summarized in United States, Department of the Army, FM 31-55, *Border Security/Anti-Infiltration Operations* (Washington, DC: United States Government Printing Office, March 1972).

25. Bonesteel interview, 328—30, 332—33.

26. FM 31-55, 3—2.

27. Bonesteel, "On Korea's DMZ," 60—61.

28. FM 31-55, 3—1.

29. Bonesteel interview, 331–32, 335.
30. Guthrie, "Korea: The Other DMZ," 17. Colonel Guthrie commanded a DMZ brigade during the height of the conflict in 1968–69. His frank account of his experiences ranks among the best sources of information during this period.
31. Staff Sergeant Richard Duke, United States Army, "Action Zone—Korea," *Army Digest* 23 (March 1968):20.
32. Guthrie, "Korea: The Other DMZ," 19. See appendix 4 of this study for a recapitulation of significant firefights involving U.S. forces.
33. Ibid., 19–20.
34. Bonesteel interview, 337.
35. Finley, *US Military Experience in Korea*, 220.
36. Staff Sergeant Richard Duke, United States Army, "Dead End for Infiltrators," *Army Digest* 23 (March 1968):21.
37. Guthrie, "Korea: The Other DMZ," 18; and "Heatless Hootches Burn Investigators," *Army Times*, 31 January 1968:7.
38. Duke, "Dead End for Infiltrators," 21; and Guthrie, "Korea: The Other DMZ," 21. There had been other, earlier fences made of barbed wire. See, for example, Colonel Robert J. Davenport, United States Army, "Barrier Along the Korean DMZ," Combat Notes column, *Infantry* 57 (May-June 1967):40–42.
39. Bonesteel interview, 333; Pruden, "Asia's Other War," 30; and Guthrie, "Korea: The Other DMZ," 22. Chain-link fence, although commonly available, costs much more per meter than barbed wire.
40. Bonesteel interview, 336–37.
41. Ibid., 332–33.
42. Guthrie, "Korea: The Other DMZ," 22; 2ID, "Operational Report . . . 30 April 1969," 1; and Robert F. Norton, "Armor Helps Defend the ROK," *Armor* 77 (September-October 1968): 19–20.
43. Finley, *US Military Experience in Korea*, 16; and Bonesteel interview, 331.
44. Bonesteel interview, 331.
45. Pruden, "Asia's Other War," 29; and Guthrie, "Korea: The Other DMZ," 18.
46. Finley, *US Military Experience in Korea*, 116–35.
47. Bonesteel, "On Korea's DMZ," 61; and Bonesteel interview, 334, 337.
48. Finley, *US Military Experience in Korea*, 116; and Guthrie, "Korea: The Other DMZ," 18.
49. Antony Preston, "The Naval War in Vietnam," in *The Vietnam War: An Almanac*, edited by John S. Bowman (New York: World Almanac Publications, 1985), 427–28.
50. FM 31-55, 7–6.
51. Ibid.
52. Institute of Strategic Studies, *The Military Balance, 1968–1969*, 38–39, 68–69.
53. Finley, *US Military Experience in Korea*, 117.
54. Bonesteel interview, 333; and Bonesteel, "U.S.-South Korean Partnership," 62.
55. Bunge, *South Korea*, 245–46.
56. Ibid., 245, 247.
57. Bonesteel, "On Korea's DMZ," 60. Note the photograph of troops from the ROK 26th Infantry Regiment aboard U.S. helicopters from I Corps (Group).
58. Bonesteel, "U.S.-South Korean Partnership," 62; Bonesteel interview, 332; and Summers, *On Strategy*, 47.

59. Bonesteel interview, 332; and Summers, *On Strategy*, 47.
60. William Loomis, "Is a Renewal of the Korean Conflict Imminent?" *DATA* 13 (June 1968):12—13. The Taebaek and Chiri Mountain areas had both experienced much guerrilla activity during the Korean War. Forces employed in these regions included portions of the U.S. 1st Marine Division. See Cable, *A Conflict of Myths*, 39—41.
61. Bunge, *South Korea*, 187—89; and Bonesteel interview, 332.
62. Bermudez, *North Korean Special Forces*, 23—26.
63. Bonesteel, "U.S.-South Korean Partnership," 63; and Kim, "North Korea's New Offensive," 178—79.

## Chapter 3

The epigraph comes from Chapin, "Success Story in South Korea," 566.

1. Finley, *US Military Experience in Korea*, 220.
2. Bermudez, *North Korean Special Forces*, 31; Bonesteel interview, 330; and Specialist Fifth Class John J. Stefans, United States Army, "Confessions of a Red Agent," *Army Digest* 23 (May 1968):17.
3. Bermudez, *North Korean Special Forces*, 32.
4. Stefans, "Confessions of a Red Agent," 19.
5. Ibid., 18—19; Guthrie, "Korea: The Other DMZ," 22; Bonesteel interview, 339—40; Bermudez, *North Korean Special Forces*, 32; United States Army, 2d Infantry Division, 1st Brigade, "Annual Historical Supplement 1968," USAMHI; and United States Army, 2d Infantry Division, 2d Brigade, "Annual Historical Supplement 1968," USAMHI.
6. Bermudez, *North Korean Special Forces*, 32—33.
7. Ibid., 32; Stefans, "Confessions of a Red Agent," 17; and Bonesteel interview, 340.
8. Bonesteel interview, 340.
9. Ibid., 340—41.
10. Ibid., 341; and Armbrister, *A Matter of Accountability*, 211—31.
11. Armbrister, *A Matter of Accountability*, 239, 261.
12. Bonesteel interview, 341; and Clark interview.
13. Johnson, *The Vantage Point*, 533.
14. Ibid., 533, 535.
15. Armbrister, *A Matter of Accountability*, 275—76.
16. Johnson, *The Vantage Point*, 535; and Armbrister, *A Matter of Accountability*, 276.
17. Armbrister, *A Matter of Accountability*, 221, 276; Chapin, "Success Story in South Korea," 561, 565; and David S. McLellan, *Cyrus Vance* (Totowa, NJ: Rowman & Allanheld, Publishers, 1985), 16.
18. Finley, *US Military Experience in Korea*, 108—9, 113—14, 116—18.
19. Chapin, "Success Story in South Korea," 565.
20. Johnson, *The Vantage Point*, 536.
21. Finley, *US Military Experience in Korea*, 118, 131; and Armbrister, *A Matter of Accountability*, 262.
22. Captain Robert P. Everett, United States Air Force, "Korea: Crisis and Response," *Airman* 12 (December 1968):5—7; Captain Robert P. Everett, United States Air Force, "Korea: Suwon—Case in Point," *Airman* 12 (December 1968):8; and Captain Robert P. Everett, United States Air Force, "Korea: A Test for Prime Beef," *Airman* 12 (December 1968):10—12.
23. Armbrister, *A Matter of Accountability*, 229—31, 266.

24. Senate, *Combat Readiness*, 6—7.
25. Vice Admiral Jerry Miller, United States Navy (ret.), "Do You Have Enough Authority?" *U.S. Naval Institute Proceedings* 116 (February 1990):69.
26. McLellan, *Cyrus Vance*, 7—15.
27. Armbrister, *A Matter of Accountability*, 276—77.
28. McLellan, *Cyrus Vance*, 16; Armbrister, *A Matter of Accountability*, 277; and Gregory Henderson, *Korea: The Politics of the Vortex* (Cambridge, MA: Harvard University Press, 1968), 142.
29. Bonesteel interview, 334—35; and Bonesteel, "On Korea's DMZ," 61.
30. "DMZ Action May Change Pay Rule," *Army Times*, 7 February 1968:1, 20; and United States, Department of the Army, AR 672-5-1, *Decorations, Awards, and Honors* (Washington, DC: United States Government Printing Office, 18 September 1989), 28.
31. "Fight Pay for Korea Due Soon," *Army Times*, 13 March 1968:1, 20; and "Korea DMZ Combat Pay Approved," *Army Times*, 10 April 1968:1, 22.
32. AR 672-5-1, 28; and United States, Department of the Army, AR 670-1, *Wear and Appearance of Army Uniforms and Insignia* (Washington, DC: United States Government Printing Office, 20 March 1987), 85, 88—89. To this day, the Commanding General, U.S. Eighth Army, retains authority to award the Combat Infantryman and Combat Medical Badges. This is the only command so authorized.
33. There were 295 official visitors during the first half of the year, during the most serious period of crisis; these included thirteen Congressional delegations, one cabinet member, twenty-seven civilian groups, and seventy-five high-level Department of Defense, service department, and military visitors.
34. Finley, *US Military Experience in Korea*, 132.
35. Jenerette, "The Forgotten DMZ," 36, quoting from the Department of Defense's "Report of the 1971 Quadrennial Review of Military Compensation."
36. Finley, *US Military Experience in Korea*, 132.
37. Everett, "Korea: Crisis and Response," 5.
38. Finley, *US Military Experience in Korea*, 122, 125.
39. Loomis, "Renewal," 13.
40. Jenerette, "The Forgotten DMZ," 40; and "Army Extends Korea Tours for Skilled," *Army Times*, 14 February 1968:3.
41. Jenerette, "The Forgotten DMZ," 40.
42. Loomis, "Renewal," 13.
43. Binder, "The Porous War," 57.
44. Ibid., 53.
45. Ibid., 57.
46. Finley, *US Military Experience in Korea*, 117, 121.
47. Ibid., 122.
48. Bonesteel, "U.S.-South Korean Partnership," 60; and Bonesteel interview, 333—34.
49. Joint Military Assistance Advisory Group (Provisional), "ROK Armed Forces Civic Action Program for 1969 (U)," 15 May 1969, 1, 9—11. This includes a summary of 1968 activities. For the older type of programs, see Kim Han Yong, *Republic of Korea Army: 1966* (Seoul: Office of Public Information, 1966), 12.
50. Bunge, *South Korea*, 86—89, 230; and Park Chung Hee, *Korea Reborn* (Englewood Cliffs, NJ: Prentice Hall, 1979), 68.
51. Bonesteel, "U.S.-South Korean Partnership," 63; and Bonesteel, "On Korea's DMZ," 60.

52. General Charles H. Bonesteel III, "Year End Press Conference—11 January 1967," in the personal papers of Colonel Clark; and "Korea Test Plan Educates Soldiers," *Army Times*, 20 March 1968:5.
53. 2ID, "Operational Report . . . 30 April 1969," 1—2.
54. Binder, "The Porous War," 55.
55. Finley, *US Military Experience in Korea*, 120—22; and Webster, "Morning Calm," 9, which indicates that the ROKs captured 1,245 agents during 1968.
56. Binder, "The Porous War," 56; and Bermudez, *North Korean Special Forces*, 33.
57. Bermudez, *North Korean Special Forces*, 33—34; and Finley, *US Military Experience in Korea*, 128.
58. Bonesteel interview, 334.

## Chapter 4

The epigraph comes from Binder, "The Porous War," 57.

1. Finley, *US Military Experience in Korea*, 128.
2. Binder, "The Porous War," 55; and Loomis, "Renewal," 12—13.
3. Stephen B. Patrick, "The East Is Red," *Strategy and Tactics* 42 (January-February 1974); 17; and Stephen B. Patrick, "The China War," *Strategy and Tactics* 47 (September-October 1979):9.
4. An, *North Korea*, 16—18.
5. Lee, "Party-Military Relations," 155, 215; and Ilpyong J. Kim, *Communist Politics in North Korea* (New York: Praeger Publishers, 1975), 76.
6. Bermudez, *North Korean Special Forces*, 68.
7. Lee, "Party-Military Relations," 155.
8. Webster, "Morning Calm," 9—10; and Bermudez, *North Korean Special Forces*, 35.
9. Lee, "Party-Military Relations," 211—16, 252—57.
10. Ibid., 155; An, *North Korea*, 18; Kim, *Communist Politics in North Korea*, 76; and Dan Oh Kong, *Leadership Chance in North Korean Politics* (Santa Monica, CA: Rand Corporation, 1988), 7. Kim Il-sung's quest for personal loyalty among key subordinates included the elevation of younger brother Kim Yong-chu and son Kim Jong-il. The latter assumed control of the KWP Propaganda and Agitation Bureau in 1971 and is now Kim Il-sung's designated successor.
11. Bermudez, *North Korean Special Forces*, 2, 12—13, 35—38, 72—73.
12. Kim, *Communist Politics in North Korea*, 76.
13. Finley, *US Military Experience in Korea*, 150; 2ID, "Operational Report . . . 1969," 2—6; and United States Army, 2d Infantry Division, "Operational Report, Lessons Learned, Headquarters, 2d Infantry Division, for Period Ending 30 April 1970 (U)," 22 September 1970, 3, hereafter cited as 2ID, "Operational Report . . . 30 April 1970."
14. United States Army, 2d Infantry Division, 2d Brigade, "Annual Historical Supplement, 1969," and United States Army, 2d Infantry Division, 3d Brigade, "Annual Historical Supplement, 1969," both in USAMHI.
15. Finley, *US Military Experience in Korea*, 129.
16. Ibid.; Bonesteel, "U.S.-South Korean Partnership," 61—63.
17. Finley, *US Military Experience in Korea*, 129.
18. Joint Military Assistance Group Korea (Provisional), "ROK Armed Forces Civic Action Program for 1969 (U)," 2—3, 11.
19. Chapin, "Success Story in South Korea," 565—66.

20. Bonesteel, "U.S.-South Korean Partnership," 61; and Bonesteel interview, 334.
21. Richard E. Bradshaw, "Major Determinants of North Korea Foreign Policy," in *The Politics of North Korea*, edited by Jae Kyu Park and Jung Gun Kim (Seoul, Korea: Kyungnam University, 1979), 190. For the first public admission of a possible change in the north, see Takashi Ota, "North Korea Held to Shift Tactics," *New York Times*, 21 September 1969:8. Ota's article offered the first public discussion of North Korean purges and a possible shift to political agitation rather than unconventional warfare. The article, based on South Korean and UNC sources, also featured the caveat that "any time the Americans present a target of opportunity, the North Koreans will seize it." Overall, it was an amazingly accurate piece of journalism. See also Bermudez, *North Korean Special Forces*, 76. Bermudez notes these other names for the 8th Special Purpose Corps: 8th Special Duties Army Group, Light Infantry Army Group, Reconnaissance Army Group, 3729th Unit, and Strategic Forces Command. This gives some clue as to the care accorded to operational security in North Korea.
22. Kim Il-song, "On Some Theoretical Problems of the Socialist Economy," in his *Revolution and Socialist Construction in Korea*, 165.
23. Lee, "Party-Military Relations," 151—59.
24. Bonesteel, "U.S.-South Korean Partnership," 63.
25. 2ID, "Operational Report . . . 30 April 1969," 2.
26. 2ID, 3Bde, "AHS 1969."
27. Finley, *US Military Experience in Korea*, 129—30.
28. 2ID, "Operational Report . . . 30 April 1969," 2—3.
29. Finley, *US Military Experience in Korea*, 130.
30. 2ID, "Operational Report . . . 30 April 1969," 2—3.
31. Bermudez, *North Korean Special Forces*, 34.
32. Richard M. Nixon, *RN, the Memoirs of Richard Nixon* (New York: Warner Books, 1978), 472—73.
33. Ibid., 473—74; and Henry Kissinger, *White House Years* (Boston, MA: Little, Brown, and Co., 1979), 317.
34. Kissinger, *White House Years*, 318—20.
35. Nixon, *RN*, 474; and United States, Congress, House, Armed Services Committee, *Inquiry Into the USS Pueblo and EC-121 Plane Incidents*, 91st Cong., 1st Sess. (Washington, DC, 28 April 1969), 924, hereafter cited as House, *Inquiry*.
36. Nixon, *RN*, 473—75.
37. Kissinger, *White House Years*, 319.
38. Nixon, *RN*, 476—77; and House, *Inquiry*, 923.
39. Kissinger, *White House Years*, 320; and Lieutenant D. L. Strole, United States Navy, and Lieutenant W. E. Dutcher, United States Naval Reserve, "Naval and Maritime Events, July 1968—December 1969," *US Naval Institute Proceedings* 96 (May 1970):14.
40. Kissinger, *White House Years*, 321.
41. Finley, *US Military Experience in Korea*, 130—31; and 2ID, 3Bde, "AHS 1969."
42. Nixon, *RN*, 488; and Finley, *US Military Experience in Korea*, 132.
43. Guthrie, "Korea: The Other DMZ," 17.
44. 2ID, "Operational Report . . . 30 April 1969," 10.
45. Finley, *US Military Experience in Korea*, 132.
46. 2ID, 3Bde, "AHS 1969."

47. United States Army, 2d Infantry Division, "Operational Report—Lessons Learned, Headquarters, 2d Infantry Division, Period Ending 31 October 1970 (U)," 1.
48. Finley, *US Military Experience in Korea*, 134.
49. Ibid., 130—35.
50. General John H. Michaelis, United States Army, "Two Decade Vigil Forges a Stronger South Korea," *Army* 20 (October 1970):60—62.

## Chapter 5

The epigraph is from United States Marine Corps, *Small Wars Manual* (Washington, DC: United States Government Printing Office, 1940), paragraph 1—16.

1. Finley, *US Military Experience in Korea*, 220.
2. Bowman, *The Vietnam War: An Almanac*, 218.
3. The casualties and duration of post-1945 American wars and military expeditions are available in R. Ernest Dupuy and Trevor N. Dupuy, *The Encyclopedia of Military History: From 3500 B.C. to the Present* (New York: Harper and Row, 1986), 1199—1400. Interestingly, the Second Korean Conflict (2 November 1966 to 3 December 1969) exceeded the Korean War in duration by one day (reckoned by U.S. Department of Defense historians to run from 27 June 1950 to 27 July 1953).
4. Finley, *US Military Experience in Korea*, 220.
5. Frederica M. Bunge, ed., *North Korea, a Country Study*, Area handbook series (Washington, DC: United States Department of the Army, 1981), 202, 223, 227.
6. Webster, "Morning Calm," 8—9.
7. James F. Dunnigan, *How to Make War: A Comprehensive Guide to Modern Warfare* (New York: William Morrow, 1988), 581.
8. Bunge, *South Korea*, 34—38, 240; and Webster, "Morning Calm," 4—5.
9. Bunge, *North Korea*, 242—45.
10. Finley, *US Military Experience in Korea*, 207.
11. Clark interview.
12. Napoleon Bonaparte, "Maxims," in *The Roots of Strategy: The 5 Greatest Military Classics of All Times*, compiled by Thomas Raphael Phillips (Harrisburg, PA: Stackpole Books, 1985).
13. Bonesteel interview, 334.
14. Perkins, "U.S. Force Structure," 242—44. U.S. forces operated independently of the country team for extended periods in Honduras (Joint Task Force Bravo, 1984 to the present), Lebanon (U.S. Multinational Force, 1982—84), and the Persian Gulf (Joint Task Force—Middle East, 1987—88), among other examples. Although not required, close liaison with the embassy was kept in all of these cases, just as in Korea during 1966—69.
15. For discussions of the challenges of combined operations, see United States, Department of the Army, FM 100-5, *Operations* (Washington, DC: United States Government Printing Office, May 1986), 164—65; and FM 100-20, 1—16 to 1—17. For an example of the committee approach in Beirut (1982—84), see Daniel P. Bolger, *Americans at War, 1975—1986: An Era of Violent Peace* (Novato, CA: Presidio Press, 1988), 198—99.
16. Bonesteel interview, 334.
17. Lieutenant Colonel A. J. Bacevich, United States Army, et al., "American Military Police in Small Wars: The Case of El Salvador," 41, typescript, March 1988, USAMHI.
18. FM 100-20, 1—11.
19. Ibid., 2—30, 5—2

20. Ibid., 2—30.
21. FM 31-55 summarizes the results of the UNC border defense operations of 1966—69. The barest summary of FM 31-55 (now out of print) can be found in the current FM 100-20, E-18 to E-20.
22. FM 100-20, 1—9.
23. Carl von Clausewitz, *On War*, translated and edited by Michael Howard and Peter Paret (Princeton, NJ: Princeton University Press, 1984), 80.
24. Finley, *US Military Experience in Korea*, 175, 185, 207, 220.
25. Bunge, *North Korea*, 128, 232, 244.
26. "Korea Today: The Vigil Continues," *Army Digest* 24 (October 1969):43—44.

# Glossary

| | |
|---|---|
| CIA | Central Intelligence Agency |
| CFC | U.S.-ROK Combined Forces Command |
| CINCUNC | Commander in Chief, United Nations Command |
| DMZ | Demilitarized Zone |
| DPRK | Democratic People's Republic of Korea |
| EUSA | U.S. Eighth Army |
| HDRF | Homeland Defense Reserve Force |
| JCS | Joint Chiefs of Staff |
| KATUSA | Korean Augmentation to the U.S. Army |
| KCIA | Korean Central Intelligence Agency |
| KIA | killed in action |
| KMAG | Korean Military Advisory Group |
| KNP | Korean National Police (south) |
| KPA | Korean People's Army (north) |
| KPAF | Korean People's Air Force (north) |
| KPN | Korean People's Navy (north) |
| KWP | Korean Workers' Party (north) |
| LIC | low-intensity conflict |
| MACV | Military Assistance Command, Vietnam |
| MDL | Military Demarcation Line |
| MIA | missing in action |
| MSR | main supply route |
| PACOM | Pacific Command |
| QRF | quick-reaction force |
| ROK | Republic of Korea |
| ROKA | Republic of Korea Army |

| | |
|---|---|
| ROKAF | Republic of Korea Air Force |
| ROKN | Republic of Korea Navy |
| SOP | standing operating procedure |
| UNC | United Nations Command |
| USAF | United States Air Force |
| USFK | United States Forces, Korea |
| USN | United States Navy |
| WIA | wounded in action |

# Bibliography

## Primary Sources

### Archival Sources

#### Combined Arms Research Library
#### United States Army Command and General Staff College
#### Fort Leavenworth, KS

Joint Military Assistance Advisory Group (Provisional). "ROK Armed Forces Civic Action Program for 1969 (U)." 15 May 1969. UNCLASSIFIED.

United States Army. 2d Infantry Division. "Operational Report—Lessons Learned, Headquarters, 2d Infantry Division, Period Ending 30 April 1969 (U)." UNCLASSIFIED.

———. "Operational Report—Lessons Learned, Headquarters, 2d Infantry Division, for Period Ending 30 April 1970 (U)." 22 September 1970. UNCLASSIFIED.

———. "Operational Report—Lessons Learned, Headquarters, 2d Infantry Division, Period Ending 31 October 1970 (U)." 14 May 1971. UNCLASSIFIED.

Webster, Everett H., Lieutenant Colonel, United States Air Force. "Is the Morning Calm About to Be Broken in Korea?" Research report no. 4471, Air War College, Air University, Maxwell Air Force Base, AL, March 1971. UNCLASSIFIED.

#### United States Army Military History Institute, Carlisle Barracks, PA

Bonesteel, Charles H., III, General, United States Army (ret.). Interview with Lieutenant Colonel Robert St. Louis. Senior Officers Oral History Program Project 73-2, 1973.

United States Army. 2d Infantry Division. 1st Brigade. "Annual Historical Supplement 1968."

United States Army. 2d Infantry Division. 2d Brigade. "Annual Historical Supplement 1968."

———. "Annual Historical Supplement 1969."

United States Army. 2d Infantry Division. 3d Brigade. "Annual Historical Supplement 1966."

———. "Annual Historical Supplement 1967."

———. "Annual Historical Supplement 1968."

———. "Annual Historical Supplement 1969."

## Other Documents

"Army Extends Korea Tours for Skilled." *Army Times*, 14 February 1968:3.

"DMZ Action May Change Pay Rule." *Army Times*, 7 February 1968:1, 20.

"DOD Order Curbs 'Premature' Medal of Honor Information." *Army Times*, 16 November 1966:5.

"Fight Pay for Korea Due Soon." *Army Times*, 13 March 1968:1, 20.

"Heatless Hootches Burn Investigators." *Army Times*, 31 January 1968:7.

"Korea DMZ Combat Pay Approved." *Army Times*, 10 April 1968:1, 22.

"Korea Test Plan Educates Soldiers." *Army Times*, 20 March 1968:5.

United States. Armed Forces Staff College. AFSC Pub 1. *The Joint Staff Officer's Guide*. Washington, DC: United States Government Printing Office, 1988.

United States. Congress. House. Armed Services Committee. *Inquiry into the USS Pueblo and EC-121 Plane Incidents*. 91st Cong., 1st Sess. Washington, DC, 28 April 1969.

United States. Congress. Senate. Committee on Armed Services. *Combat Readiness of United States and South Korean Forces in South Korea*. 90th Cong., 2nd Sess. Washington, DC, 7 June 1968.

United States. Congress. Senate. Committee on Foreign Relations. *The United States and the Korean Problem: Documents, 1943—1953*. 83d Cong., 1st Sess. Washington, DC, 1953.

United States. Department of State. "Background Notes: North Korea." Washington, DC: United States Government Printing Office, September 1968.

United States. Department of the Army. AR 670-1. *Wear and Appearance of Army Uniforms and Insignia*. Washington, DC: United States Government Printing Office, 20 March 1987.

———. AR 672-5-1. *Decorations, Awards, and Honors*. Washington, DC: United States Government Printing Office, 18 September 1989.

———. FM 31-16. *Counterguerrilla Operations*. Washington, DC: United States Government Printing Office, 19 February 1963.

———. FM 31-55. *Border Security/Anti-Infiltration Operations*. Washington, DC: United States Government Printing Office, March 1972.

_____. FM 61-100. *The Division*. Washington, DC: United States Government Printing Office, June 1965.

_____. FM 61-100. *The Division*. Washington, DC: United States Government Printing Office, November 1968.

_____. FM 100-5. *Field Service Regulations: Operations*. Washington, DC: United States Government Printing Office, 19 February 1962.

_____. FM 100-5. *Operations*. Washington, DC: United States Government Printing Office, May 1986.

_____. FM 100-15. *Field Service Regulations: Larger Units*. Washington, DC: United States Government Printing Office, 16 March 1966. With Change 1.

_____. FM 100-20. *Military Operations in Low-Intensity Conflict (Final Draft)*. Washington, DC, 7 March 1989.

_____. Table of Organization and Equipment No. 7G. *Infantry Division*. Washington, DC: United States Government Printing Office, 31 March 1966.

United States Marine Corps. *Small Wars Manual*. Washington, DC: United States Government Printing Office, 1940.


## Memoirs and Eyewitness Accounts

Binder, L. James. "On the Line in Korea: The Porous War." *Army* 19 (January 1969):50—57.

Bonesteel, Charles H., III, General, United States Army (ret.). "On Korea's DMZ: Vigil Seals the 'Porous' War." *Army* 18 (October 1968):58—61.

_____. "U.S.-South Korean Partnership Holds a Truculent North at Bay." *Army* 19 (October 1969):59—63.

Chapin, Emerson. "Success Story in South Korea." *Foreign Affairs* 47 (April 1969):560—74.

Davenport, Robert J., Colonel, United States Army. "Barrier Along the Korean DMZ." Combat Notes column. *Infantry* 57 (May-June 1967): 40—42.

Duke, Richard, Staff Sergeant, United States Army. "Action Zone—Korea." *Army Digest* 23 (March 1968):20.

_____. "Dead End for Infiltrators." *Army Digest* 23 (March 1968):21.

Everett, Robert P., Captain, United States Air Force. "Korea: A Test for Prime Beef." *Airman* 12 (December 1968):10—12.

_____. "Korea: Crisis and Response." *Airman* 12 (December 1968):5—7.

_____. "Korea: Suwon—Case in Point." *Airman* 12 (December 1968):8—9.

Guthrie, William R., Colonel, United States Army. "Korea: The Other DMZ." *Infantry* 60 (March-April 1970):17—22.

Johnson, Lyndon B. *The Vantage Point: Perspectives of the Presidency, 1963—1969.* New York: Holt, Rinehart, and Winston, 1971.

Kissinger, Henry. *White House Years.* Boston, MA: Little, Brown, and Co., 1979.

Michaelis, John H., General, United States Army. "Two-Decade Vigil Forges a Stronger South Korea." *Army* 20 (October 1970):57—62.

Miller, Jerry, Vice Admiral, United States Navy (ret.). "Do You Have Enough Authority?" Leadership Forum column. *U.S. Naval Institute Proceedings* 116 (February 1990):69—71.

Nixon, Richard M. *RN, the Memoirs of Richard Nixon.* New York: Warner Books, 1978.

Norton, Robert F. "Armor Helps Defend the ROK." *Armor* 77 (September-October 1968):18—20.

Ota, Takashi. "North Korea Held to Shift Tactics." *New York Times*, 21 September 1969:8.

Pruden, Wesley, Jr. "Asia's Other War." *Army* 17 (November 1967):26—31.

Stefans, John J., Specialist Fifth Class, United States Army. "Confessions of a Red Agent." *Army Digest* 23 (May 1968):16—19.

Westmoreland, William C. *A Soldier Reports.* Garden City, NY: Doubleday and Co., 1976.

Wicker, Rush R., Captain, United States Army. "CH-37 Mohave—Workhorse of Korea." *United States Army Aviation Digest* 14 (July 1968):32—34.

## Personal Papers

Bonesteel, Charles H., III, General, United States Army (ret.). "Year End Press Conference—11 January 1967." In the papers of Colonel Walter B. Clark, United States Army (ret.), Charleston, SC.

Crane, Paul S., M.D. "Korean Attitudes and Thought Patterns—Prepared for UNC/USFK." In the papers of Colonel Walter B. Clark, United States Army (ret.), Charleston, SC.

## Interview

Clark, Walter B., Colonel, United States Army (ret.). Telephone interview with author, Charleston, SC, 25 March 1990. Colonel Clark was the senior aide-de-camp and executive officer to General Charles H. Bonesteel III from September 1966 until August 1967.

## Other Primary Sources

Finley, James P. *The US Military Experience in Korea, 1871—1982: In the Vanguard of ROK-US Relations.* San Francisco, CA: Command Historians Office, Secretary Joint Staff, HQ, USFK/EUSA, 1983.

Kim Han Yong. *Republic of Korea Army: 1966*. Seoul: Office of Public Information, 1966.

Kim Il-song. *Revolution and Socialist Construction in Korea: Selected Writings*. New York: International Publishers, 1971.

Kim Mahn Je. *Korea's Economy: Past and Present*. Seoul, South Korea: Korea Development Institute, 1975.

Park Chung Hee. *Korea Reborn*. Englewood Cliffs, NJ: Prentice-Hall, 1979.

## *Secondary Sources*

An, Tai Sung. *North Korea in Transition: From Dictatorship to Dynasty*. Westport, CT: Greenwood Press, 1983.

Armbrister, Trevor. *A Matter of Accountability: The True Story of the Pueblo Affair*. New York: Coward McCann, 1970.

Bacevich, A. J., et al. "American Military Policy in Small Wars: The Case of El Salvador." Typescript. Carlisle Barracks, PA: United States Army Military History Institute, March 1988.

Bachtel, Charles, Colonel, United States Army (ret.). "The KATUSA Program." *Signal* 23 (December 1968):42—44.

Bermudez, Joseph S., Jr. *North Korean Special Forces*. Surrey, England: Jane's Publishing Co., 1988.

Bolger, Daniel P. *Americans at War, 1975—1986: An Era of Violent Peace*. Novato, CA: Presidio Press, 1988.

Bowman, John S., ed. *The Vietnam War: An Almanac*. New York: World Almanac Publications, 1985.

Bradley, Omar Nelson, and Clay Blair. *A General's Life: An Autobiography*. New York: Simon and Schuster, 1983.

Bunge, Frederica M., ed. *North Korea, A Country Study*. Area handbook series. Washington, DC: United States Department of the Army, 1981.

⸺. *South Korea, A Country Study*. Area handbook series. Washington, DC: United States Department of the Army, 1981.

Cable, Larry. *A Conflict of Myths: The Development of American Counterinsurgency Doctrine and the Vietnam War*. New York: New York University Press, 1986.

Clausewitz, Carl von. *On War*. Edited and translated by Michael Howard and Peter Paret. Princeton, NJ: Princeton University Press, 1984.

Davidson, Phillip B. *Vietnam at War, 1946—1975: The History*. Novato, CA: Presidio Press, 1988.

Dougan, Clark, et al., eds. *A Nation Divided. The Vietnam Experience*, vol. 20. Boston, MA: Boston Publishing Co., 1984.

Doughty, Robert A. *The Evolution of US Army Tactical Doctrine, 1946—76*. Leavenworth Papers no. 1. Fort Leavenworth, KS: Combat Studies

Institute, United States Army Command and General Staff College, August 1979.

Dunnigan, James F. *How to Make War: A Comprehensive Guide to Modern Warfare.* New York: William Morrow, 1988.

Dupuy, R. Ernest, and Trevor N. Dupuy. *The Encyclopedia of Military History: From 3500 B.C. to the Present.* New York: Harper and Row, 1986.

Halberstam, David. *The Best and the Brightest.* New York: Fawcett Crest, 1971.

Henderson, Gregory. *Korea: The Politics of the Vortex.* Cambridge, MA: Harvard University Press, 1968.

Institute for Strategic Studies. *The Military Balance, 1968—69.* London: Adlard and Son, 1968.

Jenerette, Vandon E., Major, United States Army. "The Forgotten DMZ." *Military Review* 68 (May 1988):32—43.

Kim, Ilpyong J. *Communist Politics in North Korea.* New York: Praeger Publishers, 1975.

Kim, Joungwon A. "North Korea's New Offensive." *Foreign Affairs* 48 (October 1969):166—79.

Kim, Se-jin. *The Politics of Military Revolution in Korea.* Chapel Hill: University of North Carolina Press, 1971.

Kong, Dan Oh. *Leadership Chance in North Korean Politics.* Santa Monica, CA: Rand Corporation, 1988.

"Korea Today: The Vigil Continues." *Army Digest* 24 (October 1969):41—47.

Krepinevich, Andrew F., Jr. *The Army and Vietnam.* Baltimore, MD: Johns Hopkins University Press, 1986.

Lee, Suck-Ho. "Party-Military Relations in North Korea: A Comparative Analysis." Ph.D. dissertation, George Washington University, 1983.

Loomis, William. "Is a Renewal of the Korean Conflict Imminent?" *DATA* 13 (June 1968):12—14.

McLellan, David S. *Cyrus Vance.* Totowa, NJ: Rowman & Allanheld, 1985.

"Pacific Air Forces." *Air Force and Space Digest* 51 (September 1968):83—87.

Park, Jae Kyu, and Jung Gun Kim, eds. *The Politics of North Korea.* Seoul, South Korea: Kyungnam University, 1979.

Patrick, Stephen B. "The China War." *Strategy and Tactics* 47 (September-October 1979):9

———. "The East Is Red: The Sino-Soviet War." *Strategy and Tactics* 42 (January-February 1974):4—19.

Phillips, Thomas Raphael. *Roots of Strategy: The 5 Greatest Military Classics of All Time.* Harrisburg, PA: Stackpole Books, 1985.

Shultz, Richard H., Jr., et al., eds. *Guerrilla Warfare and Counterinsurgency: U.S.-Soviet Policy in the Third World.* Lexington, MA: Lexington Books, 1989.

Simon, Jeffrey, ed. *NATO-Warsaw Pact Force Mobilization.* Washington, DC: National Defense University Press, 1988.

Stanton, Shelby L. *Vietnam Order of Battle.* Washington, DC: U.S. News Books, 1981.

Strole, D. L., Lieutenant, United States Navy, and Lieutenant W. E. Dutcher, United States Naval Reserve. "Naval and Maritime Events, July 1968—December 1969." *United States Naval Institute Proceedings* 96 (May 1970):15—96.

Summers, Harry G. *On Strategy: The Vietnam War in Context.* Carlisle Barracks, PA: United States Army War College, April 1981.

Sun Tzu. *The Art of War.* Translated and with an introduction by Samuel B. Griffith. New York: Oxford University Press, 1971.

West Point Alumni Foundation. *Register of Graduates and Former Cadets, 1969.* West Point, NY, 1969.

# LEAVENWORTH PAPERS

1. *The Evolution of US Army Tactical Doctrine, 1946—76*, Major Robert A. Doughty
2. *Nomonhan: Japanese-Soviet Tactical Combat, 1939,* by Dr. Edward J. Drea
3. *"Not War But Like War": The American Intervention in Lebanon,* by Dr. Roger J. Spiller
4. *The Dynamics of Doctrine: The Changes in German Tactical Doctrine During the First World War,* by Captain Timothy T. Lupfer
5. *Fighting the Russians in Winter: Three Case Studies*, by Dr. Allen F. Chew
6. *Soviet Night Operations in World War II,* by Major Claude R. Sasso
7. *August Storm: The Soviet 1945 Strategic Offensive in Manchuria*, by Lieutenant Colonel David M. Glantz
8. *August Storm: Soviet Tactical and Operational Combat in Manchuria, 1945,* by Lieutenant Colonel David M. Glantz
9. *Defending the Driniumor: Covering Force Operations in New Guinea, 1944,* by Dr. Edward J. Drea
10. *Chemical Warfare in World War I: The American Experience, 1917—1918,* by Major Charles E. Heller, USAR
11. *Rangers: Selected Combat Operations in World War II,* by Dr. Michael J. King
12. *Seek, Strike, and Destroy: U.S. Army Tank Destroyer Doctrine in World War II,* by Dr. Christopher R. Gabel
13. *Counterattack on the Naktong, 1950,* by Dr. William Glenn Robertson
14. *Dragon Operations: Hostage Rescues in the Congo, 1964—1965,* by Major Thomas P. Odom
15. *Power Pack: U.S. Intervention in the Dominican Republic, 1965—1966,* by Dr. Lawrence A. Yates
16. *Deciding What Has to Be Done: General William E. DePuy and the 1976 Edition of FM 100—5*, Operations, by Major Paul H. Herbert
17. *The Petsamo-Kirkenes Operation: Soviet Breakthrough and Pursuit in the Arctic, October 1944,* by Major James F. Gebhardt
18. *Japan's Battle of Okinawa, April—June 1945,* by Dr. Thomas M. Huber
19. *Scenes from an Unfinished War: Low-Intensity Conflict in Korea, 1966—1969,* by Major Daniel P. Bolger

# RESEARCH SURVEYS

1. *Amicicide: The Problem of Friendly Fire in Modern War*, by Lieutenant Colonel Charles R. Shrader
2. *Toward Combined Arms Warfare: A Survey of 20th-Century Tactics, Doctrine, and Organization*, by Captain Jonathan M. House
3. *Rapid Deployment Logistics: Lebanon, 1958*, by Lieutenant Colonel Gary H. Wade
4. *The Soviet Airborne Experience*, by Lieutenant Colonel David M. Glantz
5. *Standing Fast: German Defensive Doctrine on the Russian Front During World War II*, by Major Timothy A. Wray
6. *A Historical Perspective on Light Infantry*, by Major Scott R. McMichael
7. *Key to the Sinai: The Battles for Abu Ageila in the 1956 and 1967 Arab-Israeli Wars*, by Dr. George W. Gawrych

☆ U.S. GOVERNMENT PRINTING OFFICE: 1991 554-001/42043

www.ingramcontent.com/pod-product-compliance
Lightning Source LLC
Chambersburg PA
CBHW080545170426
43195CB00016B/2684